On the

Readers are encouraged to go to www.MissionPointPress.com
to contact the author or to find information on how to buy this book
in bulk at a discounted rate.

MISSION POINT PRESS

Published by Mission Point Press
2554 Chandler Rd.
Traverse City, MI 49696
(231) 421-9513
www.MissionPointPress.com

Photography by Michael Terrell unless otherwise noted.

ISBN: 978-1-954786-21-9
Library of Congress Control Number: 2021936969

Printed in the United States of America

ON THE TRAILS
OF NORTHERN MICHIGAN

From the *RECORD-EAGLE* columns of MICHAEL TERRELL

MISSION POINT PRESS

ON THE TRAILS OF NORTHERN MICHIGAN is your passport to some of the best hiking trails in the region, as reported by Mike Terrell in the *Traverse City Record-Eagle*.

The book covers a smorgasbord of all-season trails found in state parks and national forests, along Sleeping Bear Dunes National Lakeshore, and throughout Grand Traverse Regional Land Conservancy, Leelanau Conservancy, and Little Traverse Conservancy holdings, including some waterway river trails for kayaking and canoeing. You'll find trails that lead you to outstanding spring wildflower displays, the best sunsets, and the cool cathedrals of pine and old-growth forests to hike under during summer's heat. Hike to stunning windswept vistas of Lake Michigan, to inland lakes, forests, and river valleys. Find fall hikes that lead to colorful panoramas and winter trails that take you on a hushed day trip through snow-covered forests and fields.

MIKE TERRELL has spent over 40 years exploring the nooks and crannies around northern Michigan, writing hundreds of columns, and directing thousands of readers to trails throughout the scenic, glacier-carved landscapes around the Great Lakes.

The Terrell family

Contents

Remember: To visit Michigan state parks and DNR trails you will need to purchase the Recreation Passport.

1 // Spring

51 // Summer

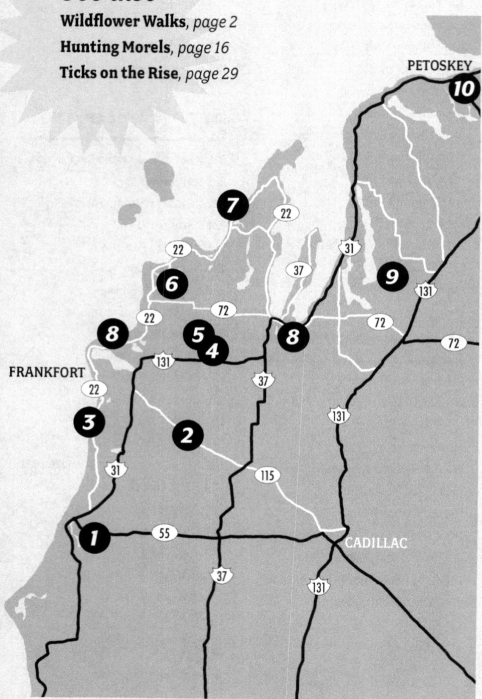

See also
Wildflower Walks, *page 2*
Hunting Morels, *page 16*
Ticks on the Rise, *page 29*

PETOSKEY

FRANKFORT

CADILLAC

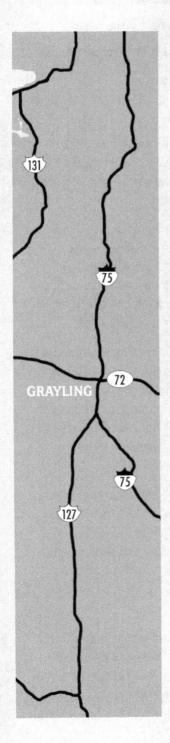

Spring

Spring can be drab and lifeless in the woods when it first arrives, and it's often accompanied by snow hiccups. But, at least it arrives, and with it the promise of better things to come outdoors.

Yes, April can be a brown, dirty month in the beginning, but promising by the end. Snowmelt leaves the sludge of winter behind, but the month's showers and warming temperatures will do much for the forest landscape. That old adage "April showers bring May flowers" is very true, and you could also add morel mushrooms into that phrase.

I've enjoyed hunting those elusive fungi for all 40 springs that I've lived up here, but this isn't a column about hunting morels. It's about some of my favorite area trails where you can count on seeing emerging spring wildflowers over the next couple of months, and, if so inclined, you might keep your eyes open for a pockmarked hooded mushroom. I have also occasionally found a few morels along the trails.

After a long, cold, winter people are looking forward to spring's longer days and warmer weather, and the spring flowers that seem to sprout overnight along trails and throughout the forest. Bunches of flowers are scattered throughout a field, stretching up hillsides. I love the striking, haphazard appeal of natural beauty. Sometimes the whole forest floor is covered with flowers, but it's a phenomenon that lasts for only a few weeks. By summer, they are mostly gone.

Most people are familiar with the showy trilliums, the signature wildflower of our northern woodlands. Other spring ephemerals are also easy to spot when you take the time to look for a little color. Blue phlox and violets, red columbines, yellow trout lilies and bellwort, and delicate, pink spring beauties are easily recognized by their bright shades. Two of my favorite white wildflowers are Dutchman's breeches and squirrel corn, because of their whimsical shapes, much like upside down breeches.

Northern Michigan's native orchards—pink, yellow, and showy lady's slippers—are woodland standouts. Two places you have a good chance of spotting them are the Leelanau Conservancy's Houdek Dunes and the Grass

River Natural Area. Look in late spring, just before summer starts, for these beauties.

Nature is jumping back to life. The ground has thawed and signs of spring are starting to emerge. Flowers will soon be blossoming. Dust off those hiking boots and head out on area trails for some spring hikes.

The Rascals said it best in their song *It's A Beautiful Morning*, which hit the airwaves over 50 years ago. "Just take in some clean fresh air, boy. No sense in staying inside, if the weather's fine and you've got the time."

Terrell's Trail Notes

Here are some of my favorite spots for spring wildflower walks, in addition to the two mentioned above.

- **Pete's Woods** is located in Arcadia Dunes Nature Preserve, off Joyfield Road. It's arguably one of the best wildflower hikes in the Grand Traverse Region. The Grand Traverse Regional Land Conservancy offers May wildflower hikes.

- **The Whaleback Natural Area's** wildflowers thrive in the microclimate on top: trillium, Dutchman's breeches, yellow violets, spring beauties, jack-in-the-pulpit, trout lilies, and periwinkle grow in abundance. There are even wild thimbleberries, which are hardly ever found in the Lower Peninsula.

- **The Grand Traverse Natural Education Reserve**, located along the banks of the Boardman River, offers several miles of trails through mixed forest, wetlands, and meadows rich in plant life and wildflowers. The Grand Traverse Conservation District routinely conducts spring wildflower hikes.

- **The Grass River Natural Area** hosts guided wildflower hikes weekly through May and June.

1

Shingle Mill Pathway

a wilderness-like outing best in spring

Looking for a place to get away from crowds for a hike?

The 10-mile Shingle Mill Pathway, located east of Vanderbilt in the 106,000-acre Pigeon River Country State Forest, is one of the great wilderness tracts in the Lower Peninsula. It's also home to the largest elk herd east of the Mississippi River. There are deer, black bear, bobcats, and reports of an occasional wolf having been spotted in the area in the past few years. You'll find a couple of drive-in campgrounds along the pathway.

The scenic, wild, rushing Pigeon River is central to much of the trail. You are alongside it throughout most of the first 3 miles, and again during the last mile. Along the way, you cross the river twice, cruise by a couple of scenic blue sinkhole lakes, some other small lakes and lily ponds, and there's a climb to a panoramic overlook of Grass Lake and views of distant hills. Spring is the best time of year to hike, when wildflowers are in abundance and ferns, which take over the trail summer and fall, are just getting started and barely visible.

Shingle Mill has several loops, and most offer views of the Pigeon River—one of the few rivers in the state to flow north. The loops range from about a mile to 10 miles. You can tailor your excursion to less than a mile, but most want a little longer exposure to this haven of peace and wilderness.

The trail is open to both hiking and mountain biking, and it is also popular with backpackers for an overnight outing at the campgrounds. A couple of times, once while cross country skiing and the other hiking in the fall, I have been fortunate enough to come across a large elk near the trail. What a thrill.

The trail is also part of the High Country Pathway, a 77-mile loop passing through four counties in the heart of the northern Lower Peninsula that offers unique opportunities for backpackers. It passes through several bogs and swamps on the north end.

Terrell's Trail Notes

🪧 In Vanderbilt, head east on Sturgeon Valley Road about ten miles to the trailhead parking area—it's on the right, just after crossing the Pigeon River. The trail begins at the back of the campground across the road.

🪧 There are three small loops that total about a mile and a half between signposts 1 and 4, much of it along the river. For the long loop, head towards signposts 5 from 3—those lead to the 6- and 10-mile loops. The trail heads away from the river for a while. It climbs a wooded ridgeline, passing by the Pigeon River Country Forest headquarters—which has some interesting displays if it's open—before dropping down through another campground. There, the trail crosses the river on a bridge. Campers have created a pool over a period of time by stacking up rocks.

🪧 The six-mile loop breaks off here at signpost 6. The trail climbs a steep ridge and rejoins the long trail at signpost 12, after heading across the highlands for a little over a mile and a half. For the long loop, head over to signpost 7. Continue through post 8 towards post 9 on the 10-mile loop. You have a long, steep climb to post 10 after passing Grass Lake. A short side spur at the top leads to a panoramic view looking out over the Grass Lake valley and distant hills 20 miles away. It makes a great place to sit on the bench and enjoy the eye-pleasing view while catching your breath. At least that's what I do.

🪧 At post 11, the High Country Pathway loop heads north and you head on around to post 12. Along the way, you pass a couple of beautiful, small lakes that often contain beaver lodges. It's a little over a mile from the end when you head on from post 12. Near the end, you will encounter a long, wooden walkway, about two-tenths of a mile, over an extensive bog.

2

Betsie River Pathway

ride or hike

The Betsie River Pathway in southern Benzie County is a great place for an easy, scenic hike down to the Betsie River, and it's a great place to look for morel mushrooms in the spring. It's also popular with mountain bikers.

There are three, east-side loops available, ranging from 3.6 to 5 miles—most of it flat, with a couple of small, easy up-and-down hill treks. I ran into a family with small kids mountain biking the trail.

"This is a great pathway for my six- and eight-year-old kids," explained Grand Haven resident Rob Brown. "I rode it this morning, coming over from Crystal Mountain, which is a bit long for the kids to ride.

The Betsie River name comes from the French for "la rivière aux Bec-scies," meaning "river of sawbill ducks."

"But, I thought this would be a great woodland trail for them to experience and easy enough for them to handle. So we just drove over to the trailhead parking lot from the resort and took them around the three-mile loop. They love the ride."

The first five miles of the pathway is a fairly gentle ride, meandering across open meadows, through pine and hardwood forests. No great overlooks, but it envelops you in a northern Michigan woodland. It's also a pleasant, relaxing stroll. You have no idea that one of northern Michigan's prime resorts is less than a mile from the Department of Natural Resources (DNR) trail.

There's close to 3 miles on the other side of Longstreet Road that passes through an old, abandoned orchard before entering the forest and plunging down to the banks of the Betsie River. It's a little harder to hike down to the river and back up, but very scenic and woodsy.

The Pathway is a beautiful area of constantly changing cover, from hardwoods to sweet-smelling pine stands, and open, often wildflower-filled meadows in spring. I've spotted deer, turkey, and ruffed grouse, and heard coyotes yelping in early evening during summer's long daylight hours.

Terrell's Trail Notes

T The trailhead is located off M-115. Follow King Road a short distance to Longstreet Road and head south for about a mile. I like hiking the trail counterclockwise. From the trailhead, head south to post 2. At that post, you have a choice of heading over to post 5 for a about a 3.5-mile hike back to the trailhead. Heading around to post 3 through 4 to 5 will net you a 5-mile hike. You pass a marked Crystal Mountain connector trail along the way.

T Some of the area through this section has been logged recently and is growing back. They did a good job of protecting the pathway by leaving trees along it, and the more open area allows you to get a good look at the terrain. It's about two miles from post 5 back to the trailhead.

T To ride or hike down to the river, cross Longstreet Road, and it's a short distance through an old orchard to post 6. Continue straight ahead into the forest as the trail drops towards the river in a little over a half mile. At post 9, you can head right and avoid the last trek down to the river. Either way, it's less than a quarter mile to post 8, and I like going down along the river before climbing back out of the valley. It's a hike of 2.7 miles. If you do the whole pathway, it's 7.7 miles.

T I often see cars with bike racks at the trailhead parking area, but seldom run into mountain bikers out on the trail. The secluded pathway is well worth the trip for a ride or hike. Most of my morels were found in the woods along the trail between signposts 1 and 5.

3

Pete's Woods Trail

wildflowers in spades

One of my favorite spring wildflower hikes is Pete's Woods Trail at Arcadia Dunes in Benzie County. At times, you almost feel like you're hiking through a garden, but the hilly, wooded landscape reminds you that you're in northern Michigan.

Located in a remote corner of Arcadia Dunes Nature Preserve, the trail's off Joyfield Road, which you would take to get to either the Old Baldy Trails overlooking Lake Michigan or the single-track at Dry Hill for mountain biking. Pete's Woods is about 4 miles from Lake Michigan, as the crow flies.

Squirrel corn at Pete's Woods.

You won't find great overlooks from huge sand dunes or long trails to hike and mountain bike, but in springtime I've always found an abundance of wildflowers carpeting the forest floor. It's arguably, in my opinion, one of the best wildflower hikes you'll find in the Grand Traverse Region. Despite the hilly topography, it's not a hard hike—only a little over a mile and a half long. It gives you ample time to just mosey along and be amazed at all the wildflowers you will see blanketing the hills.

There's a wide variety of blooms to view: spring beauties, Dutchman's breeches, squirrel corn, yellow trout lily, bellwort, and, of course, trillium. I've also found a few morels residing among the wildflowers and leaves. I know they don't want you picking the wildflowers, but I assume morels are all right—at least I hope so.

The best times I've found for viewing is from May through the first couple of weeks in June. Take Swamp Road off Joyfield, and it's about a half mile on the dirt road to the parking area for the trailhead.

The trail and preserve is named for Pedro Rodríguez, who homesteaded the farm fields you drive by on Swamp Road. He also owned the forested ravines where the trail is located, and he planted the red and white pines you hike through to begin the trail. He and his wife, Iva, owned the farm from 1928 to the 1970s when Consumers Power purchased the land. The Grand Traverse Regional Land Conservancy permanently protected Arcadia Dunes and Pete's Woods in 2005.

The trail isn't hard. Pick a sunny day, wear some comfortable walking shoes, bring your camera, and be prepared for an almost magical experience. The wildflowers, when in full bloom, are a stunning sight in Pete's Woods.

Terrell's Trail Notes

🐾 From the trailhead parking area, you quickly cross one of Rodríguez's old farm fields and pass through the pines he planted. As you begin the climb up the forested hills, you reach the junction for the loop trail. I like to go right—west—on the loop, because this is where the most brilliant display of wildflowers occurs. The trail continues to gradually climb through the forest, which you probably won't notice if the wildflowers are blooming.

🐾 Climbing up the western flank of hills, which gets the long hours of a warm afternoon sun, the wildflowers seem to take over the forest floor and ascending hills. After a while, the trail swings to the south, eventually east, then north as it heads back to the trailhead. You still see some wildflowers, but not the dazzling display you saw on the western flank.

🐾 This is where you suddenly realize how far you have climbed. At about the halfway point around, the loop trail swings north along the top of the hill, then abruptly back west. At that point, you can look down into a deep hollow between hills. Well over 100 feet below, you can see Swamp Road meandering through the hollow. From this point, you proceed around the top of the hill and start back down to the trailhead.

🐾 This trail is also pretty in the fall when the hardwood forest turns colorful.

Spring walks bring hope...
and morel mushrooms

Photo: Adobe Stock

Who doesn't like spring as we rid ourselves of winter?

I love hiking in the woods this time of year. Things start to green. The forest floor blooms with new life. It's a time of hope, new beginnings, and inspiration, as the poets eloquently wax.

For me and thousands of others, it's the beginning of a new morel mushroom season. My hope is that it brings forth many woodland fungi, which inspires me to spend more time stalking my favorite hunting area.

It's normally just a great time to be in the northern Michigan woodlands. Temperatures have warmed enough to feel comfortable. You don't have to feel hurried against chill winds and cold. I look forward to slow walks through the woods with my mesh bag and a walking stick that I've named Gandalf. It has a head with a sorcerer's cap carved on one end of a thick oak stick. I've had it for over 30 years. It makes a great poking stick for moving twigs and leaves around when searching for those little woodland delicacies.

With an eye to the ground it's a good time—at least for me—to reflect on past mushroom hunts with family. My wife, Kathy, who passed away nearly 20 years ago, used to love this time of year and the spring hunts. Our children would spend time hunting with us on weekends. It's great family time and a wonderful way to introduce them to outdoor activities. Kids are naturally curious, normally have great eyesight, and the fact that they are closer to the ground gives them an advantage in spotting morels.

My mother and father passed on the tradition to my siblings and me, even though we grew up in Indiana, which doesn't have the tradition of mushroom hunting that we have in northern Michigan. My parents would take trips to the Wolverine State in the spring for hunts. Those were always great family outings. We stayed in cabins and spent days foraging in the woods.

That tradition draws thousands of people, many from other nearby states, into our woods during the month of May. Most people are pleasant, as long as you don't ask them where they found the bounty they may be carrying. That's one secret most mushroom hunters will carry to the grave. Be vague, try to find a secluded area, and enjoy the hunt. Remember: it's a great time of year for a walk in the woods; finding a stash of morels is just a nice bonus.

Terrell's Mushroom Hunting Tips

🍄 Mushroom hunting is a visual experience. Walk slowly, keeping your eyes on the ground, and look for that rumpled cone poking through leaves and twigs. It helps to have something to poke around gently. Take a woven mesh bag (such as an orange or potato bag) with you to put your finds in. This is extremely important because morels spread through spores, which shake loose as they are jostled about. Allowing the spores to fall to the ground will help to ensure morel hunting for our grandchildren and beyond.

🍄 Before trekking off into the woods, the novice would be well advised to check out morel mushrooms on the internet. Find pictures and helpful information on identification. The best way is to go with a seasoned mushroom hunter the first few times.

🍄 Morels are fairly easy to identify; probably one of the easiest mushrooms. They all have the same hollow stalk with a hooded, sponge-like pitted head attached. Some are black, some gray, and some white or yellow in color. If the bottom of the hood is attached to the stem, it's a true morel, which is what you want to stick with. There are false morels —best avoided—that are easily identified, because the bottom of the hood is not attached to the mushroom.

Photo: Adobe Stock

▼ Stands of aspen and ash trees and around dead elms, spruce stumps, and old, abandoned orchards are some of the more likely spots to check. Some areas where I've enjoyed good hunts in the past are woodlands off the Vasa, Muncie Lakes, and Betsie River Pathways; the wooded hills of Antrim and Leelanau Counties; and the hills above Empire, Mesick, and Yuba. The rest is up to you.

▼ Once you find some morels, cut the stem cleanly just above the ground. Keep them out of the sun and as well aired as possible until processing, which should be done as soon as you get home. If you're eating them right away, cut them in half, wash them, and follow your favorite recipe.

▼ I eat some and dry as many as possible to rehydrate and eat all year long. Some people freeze them in various ways, but I've found that when you reconstitute dried morels in very hot water they taste almost fresh when prepared.

4

Lake Dubonet

renew your soul and spirit

Looking for a great spot for a quiet paddle—seclusion with an undeveloped shoreline—where you are almost assured of seeing a variety of wildlife and waterfowl?

Lake Dubonet fills that bill. I guarantee that spending an hour or two quietly paddling around this serene 1000-acre lake will renew your soul and spirit.

"It's like a little piece of northern Canada tucked away in northern Michigan," Jim DuFresne, an outdoor writer who summers in Elk Rapids, told me a few years ago. "It's a pretty special place for paddling, fishing, and wildlife viewing."

The lake was created in 1956 when the Platte River, a small stream at this point flowing through two small lakes, was dammed to create one large lake that would improve fishing, waterfowl habitat, and recreational use. It more than doubled the size of the two small lakes. There's now a state forest campground on one shore and a rustic campground on the opposite shore to accommodate hikers and equestrians. The Shore-to-Shore Trail for horseback riders passes through the area, and there is a 7-mile loop trail—the Lost Lake Pathway—that meanders along the lake and river and through the Pere Marquette State Forest, which hikers and mountain bike riders enjoy.

The lake has one home tucked into an inlet on the shore opposite from the launch site, which is part of the campground. You can't see it until you paddle by. Otherwise, the shoreline is undeveloped, and you don't see the campground when paddling around the large lake, providing a real sense of seclusion.

The north end of the lake, covered with an old "ghost" forest, offers some interesting paddling as you work your way through the silent, gray trunks and small islands created by the flooding. There's even a floating island. One of the islands has a large eagle nest high up in a tree.

On a recent morning paddle with friends from the Traverse Area Paddling Club, we could hear the eaglets chirping in the nest, but didn't see them or their parents. I have seen the eagles soaring high over the lake in the past. We were also able to observe a nesting pair of loons that have resided here for years with a couple of chicks in tow on the lake. We kept our distance so they wouldn't be disturbed. When paddling in the early evening, I've often heard their eerie, yodel-like call, echoing across the lake. It's the call of the wild. Deer can often be spotted in the evening as well, coming down to the lake for a drink along the shore.

As you paddle around the lake, notice the flooded timber, lily pads, and thick clusters of weeds scattered throughout—these are hot spots for fish. It's a popular stop for local fishers. Northern pike, perch, and muskie are a few of the species that call this lake home, as well as monster-sized hybrid bluegills in the early spring and an impressive population of largemouth bass, according to the DNR. Keep a respectful distance from the fishers.

It's an interesting area for outdoor enthusiasts. Close to Traverse City and not far off busy U.S. 31, the lake and the pathway offer solitude and a quiet escape.

Terrell's Trail Notes

⊤ To access the boat launch on the lake, take Gonder Road off U.S. 31, which runs by Interlochen Golf Course. When you come to the dirt road, continue straight and follow it to the launch area. There's plenty of parking available.

5

Ransom Lake Natural Area

under the radar

The Ransom Lake Natural Area, just southeast of the village of Lake Ann, offers an easy, scenic hike of around 2.5 miles along a beautiful, quick-flowing creek and around the small lake.

The 220-acre natural area has been around since the early 2000s, but on my first hike here, I had the feeling that it wasn't a large area. For that reason, I think it flies under the radar of many area hikers. That's a mistake, as I discovered.

A bridge crosses swift-flowing Ransom Creek as it exits the lake rushing towards Lake Ann.

There are two trailheads—one off Bellows Lake Road that comes off CR 610 and the other off CR 665. From the trailheads, you have an out-and-back trail of about a half mile that hooks up with a trail of 1.4 miles around the lake. I like the southern trailhead off CR 665, or Lake Ann Road as locals know it, that follows Ransom Creek up to the lake. To me, it's more scenic than the woodland trail from the trailhead off Bellows Lake Road.

My first thought as I hiked along the creek trail was, "This is the essence of a northern Michigan hike." A swift-flowing creek tumbles through a valley between ridges as it rushes from an isolated, beautiful small lake surrounded by a northern Michigan forest. As soon as you leave the trailhead parking lot, following the pathway along the creek, you leave behind any road noise and signs of civilization. It was only the sounds of birds chirping and the creek bubbling just below the trail.

Then the first hint of buzzing in my ear let me know that mosquitoes were present, and in short order they would have been all over me if I hadn't applied bug spray before leaving the parking area. I was mostly alright, but they were so annoying that I ended up swallowing a couple before I realized that my mouth should stay shut.

I have noticed, since the weather finally warmed up in May, that the mosquitoes have been the worst I've seen in recent years. They seem to be everywhere in the woods, not just near water. Ticks have been late showing up, but recent posts on Facebook from friends would indicate they are also out and looking for blood. They are expected to continue to be bad, which unfortunately seems to be the norm.

A friend who went hiking—dressed properly with long pants, socks pulled up over pants and fully covered—discovered ticks on her when she got home to take a shower. She had undressed in a mudroom before entering the house and discovered the ticks in her bathroom the next morning.

Take precautions and check yourself closely after coming in from a hike.

Despite the insects, this area provides a pleasant spring hike when wildflowers are up, especially the marsh marigolds. Don't forget the bug repellent.

Terrell's Trail Notes

T There are two trailheads—both are about a half mile, one way, joining the pathway that circles the lake, which is about 1.4 miles around, according to my fitness tracker. Total distance around the lake and the out-and-back paths from the trailheads is about a 2.5-mile hike. I find that the out-and-back trail along Ransom Creek is the most scenic way in and out. When you reach the lake, a picturesque wooden bridge crosses the creek to begin the trail around the lake.

T Benches made by local Boy Scout troops have been placed along the pathway at scenic locations and an attractive fishing dock with benches is also near the creek crossing. It's also a great place to just sit and enjoy the view—when the mosquitoes die off. The trail that leads to Ransom Lake along the creek is considered a universally accessible (UA) trail. It joins the lake circle, and the fishing dock can also be reached via that trail. Only the out-and-back trail along the creek is UA, not the trail circling the lake.

Ticks on the rise

Ticks are arriving earlier in the spring and, as always, hunting for blood. This is something hikers need to prepare for as the new normal.

"A mild winter allows ticks to remain active, especially in the western Michigan counties along the lakeshore. We will start getting reports in February of active ticks in the southwestern counties," said Howard Russell, a Michigan State University entomologist, when I spoke with him recently. "The blacklegged tick, which carries Lyme disease, is present in all of the counties along Lake Michigan, and it's only going to get worse."

The Centers for Disease Control and Prevention (CDC) reports over 1,200 confirmed cases of Lyme disease in Michigan since 2001. Due to the fact that the CDC's data only represent confirmed cases, the actual quantity of Lyme disease cases may be far greater, and they estimate a total of 9,696 true cases in Michigan. It can be a hard disease to detect and is often misdiagnosed.

Lyme disease is not something you want to mess around with. Typical symptoms include fever, headache, fatigue, and rash. If left untreated, infection can spread to joints, heart, and the nervous systems. If you get any of these symptoms after visiting a known tick habitat, make an appointment to visit your health provider immediately.

"It's hard to explain the sudden explosion of ticks, but the possibilities have always been there," explained Russell, considered one of the leading experts on the subject. "Ticks have long been established along the East Coast and upper Midwest in Minnesota and Wisconsin. Birds are the most likely culprit in bringing them in, and they'll continue to spread eastward across the Lower Peninsula."

Ticks love sandy areas with varied plant life, which is typical of all counties along Lake Michigan. They go through three life stages: larva, nymph, and adult. Each stage needs blood meals, according to Russell.

"They are shifty little creatures and perch on plants and branches waiting for a host to brush by for its blood meal. [Then] it falls off, evolves, and looks for its next host," he explained. "Ticks are not born carrying Lyme disease,

Tick on a blade of grass.
(Photo by Mcvoorhist)

but instead contract it in the larvae stage, feeding on infected animals, such as deer—and especially mice. Ticks can take two or three years to evolve through the three stages, with the larger nymph stage most likely to pass the disease along to humans.

"They survive the winters with leaf cover and snow serving as an insulating blanket, and the milder winters are helping their numbers to explode. I expect the problem to become worse, not better, in future years now that they are here," Russell concluded.

If you are like me, you aren't going to quit going outside for hikes and mountain bike rides through our woodlands and grasslands. Precaution is the reasonable way to go.

Wearing long-sleeve shirts, long pants, and socks that you can tuck your pants into is good advice. Spraying with a bug repellent exposed skin that contains at least 30 percent DEET will help, and treating clothing and camping gear with products containing the insecticide permethrin will also help greatly. The insecticide can't be sprayed on exposed skin, but spraying it once on clothing and equipment will last for several outings, according to Russell.

"One of the important things people can do after coming home is to check yourself over from head to toe and take a shower," Russell advised. "You're looking for something that is minuscule, sometimes no bigger than the head of a pin. Prompt removal is essential. It only takes 24 to 48 hours for Lyme disease to be transmitted."

Local veterinarians advise giving dogs tablets to prevent ticks and fleas, and also a Lyme disease vaccination. The tablets kill the pests if they try and attach; the shot will prevent the disease even if the dog is bitten before the tick falls off.

6

Kettles Trail

unique topography within the National Lakeshore

The Kettles Trail, which opened in 2019 in the Bows Lake region of the Sleeping Bear Dunes National Lakeshore, offers a unique glacial topography that includes many kettle bogs and lakes. The distinct terrain is atypical of the many other hiking trails located in the National Lakeshore, which mostly highlight beaches, sand dunes, and picturesque overlooks of Lake Michigan.

It does offer an eye-catching display of May wildflowers that I discovered hiking it in the spring. The rest of the year the kettle formations take center stage, which offer overlooks of deep kettles and kettle bogs.

The area contains over a dozen of the distinct kettle formations, which were caused by huge blocks of ice left behind by the last retreating glacier some 11,000 years ago. When the ice blocks—covered with moraines—melted, numerous kettle holes were left, which disrupted the landscape, leaving behind a jumbled, rugged topography of ridges and mounds. This is the best example of the glacially created landforms in Michigan.

Some of the climbs are long and, at times, steep. Elevation change is nearly 200 feet between the low point on the trail system and the trailhead parking lot. The trail, which has some backtracking, is close to 3.5 miles in length, if you hike the entire system. The southern half of the system offers moderate hiking with a couple of more difficult areas, but the northern loop is more challenging, with a long climb and a narrow, winding descent. In winter, snowshoeing would probably be the best way to explore. Regular cross country skiing would be difficult; backcountry skiing may be easier. Some of the trail is close to a 25 percent grade.

I highly recommend this trail system for a springtime hike. The first quarter mile of trail from the trailhead is a UA pathway to an overlook down into a kettle. In early springtime or late fall, you can glimpse into the depths of a kettle without leaves obscuring your view. The best time is early May before leaves have fully formed and wildflowers are in abundance.

Terrell's Trail Notes

T The main trail leads off of the UA trail and winds down through a meadow entering the forest below. After a half a mile, the quarter-mile bog spur takes off to the right. The spur trail takes you down to the edge of an expansive kettle bog with a new deck hanging over the edge offering great views. The bog almost looks like a small lake. A kettle becomes a bog when the only source of water is precipitation and the closed water ecosystem turns acidic due to decomposing plant matter. Not all kettles are bogs; some have fresh water. You pass a couple of other kettles on the way to the bog overlook.

T The main trail continues along an old two-track that's relatively flat. Hills rise up on both sides, which are carpeted in wildflowers in spring and early summer. A little over a mile along the main trail, you come to the beginning of the rugged mile-long loop trail that climbs nearly 150 feet in elevation. You can do the loop in either direction. I like following the loop to the left. The two-track is a more gradual climb to the top of the loop. When a single-track trail exits the two-track and starts back down, it reminds me of hiking on trails in the Blue Ridge Mountains with narrow, winding, and jaw-dropping views into steep kettles where you can't see a bottom.

T However, before the loop trail leaves the two-track, continue following it a short distance. It runs into the end of Lanham Road and continues up a ridge for a short distance to the right. Along that ridge, you catch glimpses of the rugged terrain of kettles and ridges to the north, which is where more park land may be added in the future as it becomes available. When you reach the end of the loop trail, retrace the trail to the trailhead parking lot.

7

Whaleback

**"Got a whale of a tale
to tell ya lads, a whale of
a tale or two, 'bout the
flappin' fish and the girls
I've loved on nights like
this with the moon above."**

That strand from a song performed by Kirk Douglas in *20,000 Leagues Under the Sea* frequently comes to mind when hiking Leelanau County's Whaleback Natural Area. It was one of my favorite movies as a young lad, and it's the only song I know about whales. It always fired up my imagination, and maybe that's why.

Spring beauties

A brooding, humpbacked mound of land, Whaleback rises over 300 feet above Lake Michigan and is one of the most recognized features along the Leelanau shoreline. It has long fired the imagination of local residents.

One of the largest, undeveloped shoreline tracts in the county, the natural area encompasses close to 40 acres and a half a mile or so of pristine Lake Michigan shoreline. The Leelanau Conservancy acquired an interest in the property a couple of decades ago, and created the natural area in 1996.

It's not one of the conservancy's larger holdings, but it's one of the most frequently visited, according to staff. That's despite the fact that the parking lot—off M-22, just south of Leland and Whaleback Inn—only holds about six vehicles. Village residents will walk over and make the climb.

It's not a long trail—a little over a mile with about a half a mile of steep climbing. Once on top, you have a nice three-quarter mile loop trail and an observation deck offering picturesque views of Good Harbor Bay, Pyramid Point, and the Manitou Islands. The trail on top continues along the bluff, reaching a point where you have a limited overlook of Leland beaches, before returning to the trail you came up on.

I've been there in early May when thick fog moves up the deep, finger-like ravines from Lake Michigan and breaks over the top of Whaleback. Standing on the observation deck, I could only see the distant top of Pyramid Point on the other side of the bay. Wisps of fog moving up the bluff provide an almost ethereal experience. I could imagine ancient sailors using the Whale as a reference point for the mainland.

The top is covered by a second-growth hardwood forest: maple, beech, red oak, white ash, cedar, and even some ironwood. The larger trees are probably close to a century old, and some of the oldest are along the top of the bluff. They may not appear as big, but harsh conditions with wind and exposure stunts their growth.

The canopy also shelters the bald eagles that nest here. You occasionally see them from the observation platform, flying over the bay along the bluff.

Wildflowers do very well in the micro-climate on top— trilliums, Dutchman's breeches, yellow violets, spring beauties, jack-in-the-pulpit, trout lilies, and periwinkle grow in abundance. There are even wild thimbleberries, which are hardly ever found in the Lower Peninsula. Normally these flowers are found along the Lake Superior coastline, which tells you something about the harsh conditions they prefer.

Terrell's Trail Notes

🚩 Glacial Hill Trail, the main trail on this glacial moraine, left behind 11,000 years ago by the last retreating glacier, steadily climbs to the top. It's fairly steep, but the views from the top are worth the climb. Stay on the trail as some of it crosses private property. There's a bench about halfway up that provides a nice rest from the climb. You come back down the same way.

🚩 A sign near the top alerts that you are now in the natural area, and it's also where a loop trail on top reconnects with the main trail. Follow the main trail up to the observation deck perched on the edge of the bluff. You'll be rewarded with spectacular views. After spending time enjoying the overlook, follow the trail left along the bluff to another overlook of the shoreline leading to Leland. A loop brings you back around to the main trail, which you follow back down. Trails are very distinguishable and easy to follow.

8

Boardman and Platte

pedal to paddle

A beautiful, sunny spring day is forecast, and you decide it's perfect for that first float down an area river. But, you can't find a friend to coordinate a shuttle with.

One way I've found of getting around falls back on another longtime passion—biking. By combining the two outdoor activities—a pedal and paddle— I get a good workout and a lot of flexibility for river paddling. I don't have to rely on a group outing or matching schedules with others, and it allows me to go on the spur of the moment, taking advantage of that sunny day. I just throw my bike and kayak or canoe on the vehicle and go.

Two of the best area rivers for this type of activity are the Boardman and Lower Platte; both offer easy access points for spotting a vehicle and kayak or canoe, with a short bike ride between.

The Boardman is close to home, and it allows several choices for pedal and paddle opportunities. Paddling the upper portion from The Forks, with its nice put-in just a half a mile south of Supply Road down to Scheck's Forest Campground, or on to the Brown Bridge takeout, offers a float through a valley of high banks and heavily forested terrain with few cottages. The river ranges in size from 20 to 40 feet with a moderate to quick current. I never get tired of paddling this section.

You utilize Brown Bridge Road (dirt) from The Forks, which crosses the river at Scheck's and continues on to the Brown Bridge landing. It's a little under 7 miles, with Schecks about halfway. The river float is around the same distance. You will need a mountain bike.

If you go later in the afternoon, you will often find deer coming down to the river for a drink. If you are quiet, it isn't hard to slip up on them. I've floated around a corner and been almost face-to-face with them.

You can also put-in at Brown Bridge Landing and paddle down to the Shumsky Road public access. There are several

stretches of undeveloped land along this portion of the river, but cottages, homes, and private bridges crossing the river are frequent. Despite the homesteads, which pass quickly, it's still a scenic float. You take a small portion of Brown Bridge Road and River Road to reach Shumsky. It's 4 miles and all paved. The river float in this case is longer at around 6 miles.

Another favorite pedal and paddle combo offers a float down the scenic Lower Platte River through low dunes to Lake Michigan. The bike ride on an all-paved road is short—around 2.5 miles—and the float trip is about 4 miles. This tranquil float passes through the National Park on its way to the big lake. The shallow river valley—mostly 2 to 5 feet deep—passes through a small lake and hardwood hills before entering a stretch of small sand dunes prior to reaching the Lake Michigan. The normally slow current is almost nonexistent in the spring during high lake levels.

Terrell's Trail Notes

▼ Summer can be busy with float traffic, including lots of tubers. Also, Riverside Canoes will be starting float trips, which can almost clog the river. Springtime or fall is best to paddle the river. I like to use the convenient township parking area and take-out. The cost for using their lot is $5. I use the National Lakeshore put-in, though, which is quite nice and has a rack where you can lock your bike. On the Boardman trips, I hide the bike in nearby woods, locking it securely to a large tree.

9

Grass River Natural Area

outdoor exploration and education

"Stay on the boardwalks and out of the mud," Whitney Campbell, an Indiana mother visiting the Grass River Natural Area, sternly warned her children as they explored the natural area along the river through wetlands.

"My family has been coming up to the Torch Lake area for years during the summer, and we always find time to take a trip to Grass River. It's interesting and offers some great hiking opportunities. The kids like the boardwalks and seeing the waterfowl. This morning, they got to watch one of those bug-eating plants do its thing, which got them excited," she laughed.

Nature trails, wildlife, waterfowl, and lots of swamp, marshland, and bogs to explore and learn about—that's what Antrim County's Grass River Natural Area (GRNA) is all about.

The good news is that you won't have to be knee deep in black ooze to explore this wonderful, interesting natural area that borders the Grass River between Lake Bellaire and Clam Lake. There are plenty of boardwalks to keep your socks dry and shoes clean.

When developers began filling wetlands along the short river in the 1960s in preparation for building, it prompted fundraising efforts among county residents to purchase the land. It was dedicated as a natural area in 1977.

It seems like they've been adding boardwalk ever since. Some trails are all boardwalk, and the way they twist, turn, and snake through wetlands make you feel as if they go on forever. Actually, there is close to 1.5 miles of boardwalk. Kids love them, and so do their parents; they keep the kids dry and clean while exploring the area. There's a total of 7 miles of trails between the upland forest trails and the boardwalks snaking through the floating sedge and wetlands.

GRNA is one of the state's premier nature preserves. It protects over 1,400 acres and attracts more than 15,000 visitors annually. It borders much of the Grass River with over 6 miles of shoreline. There are 400 species of plants, 49 species of mammals and 147 species of birds that have been inventoried within its borders. It even offers a short perception pathway that is wheelchair and stroller accessible for visitors with special needs and the visually impaired. Plaques explaining the habitat along the pathway are also in braille.

The focus of the organization is protecting the watershed, education, and providing access to this wonderful natural area with opportunities to learn more. Classes are scheduled on many weekends throughout the summer and educational hikes

on many weekdays. There are over 80 summer classes offered, and many are free. GRNA provides a wetlands curriculum to over 1,200 area schoolchildren each year.

Terrell's Trail Notes

- The Grass River Natural Area is located off CR 618, a half a mile west of the M-88 intersection between Alden and Mancelona. There is a large map sign in the parking lot with marked intersections, directional arrows, and maps. You can also download a trail map from the website, www.grassriver.org.

- The Chippewa, Nipissing, and Algonquin Trails—totaling 2.5 miles—take off from the west side of the parking lot, right behind the large trail map. They meander through upland forests and meadows.

- The Woodland and Wildfire Trails combine for about a 2-mile walk through wetlands and an upland forest. You cross swift-flowing Finch Creek three times on the outing, a very scenic route.

- The Sage Meadow Trail and other boardwalk trails begin behind the new Grass River Center building, which offers educational material, displays, and items for sale to benefit the natural area. Boardwalks will lead you down to the river with numerous overlooks and through the sage meadow. Numbered posts identify plants and more information can be found in the trail guide. This is where the bug-eating pitcher plants are located, always a favorite with the kids.

- You may spot marsh hawks, ospreys, or bald eagles circling overhead above the large marsh. Wildlife you might see from the low observation towers out by the river includes river otters, mink, and white-tailed deer. Bobcats—although you probably won't see any—also live in the area. Dawn and dusk are the best times to visit for wildlife viewing. The natural area is open from dawn to dusk year-round.

10

Bear River Valley

Petoskey's Bear River Valley Recreation Area, oh my: whitewater, falls, trails, a great spot for hikers, bikers, and kayakers to try

The 1.5-mile-long Bear Valley Recreation Area—which splits Petoskey down the middle— is a natural beauty located just 2 blocks from the city's famed Gaslight District. The 36-acre park, which the Bear River flows through, features steep terrain, unpaved and paved trails, boardwalks, woods, and open meadows.

You can hike, bike, fish, picnic, nature watch, and go whitewater kayaking in the Whitewater Park on the Bear River. It's a real boon for outdoor enthusiasts.

The Bear has the biggest drop over its last mile of any Lower Peninsula river. It drops nearly 80 feet as it rushes from the highlands to Little Traverse Bay, providing the perfect environment for a whitewater park. Opened in 2010, it has drops and rapids from Class I to Class III and over a dozen features to challenge paddlers. The park was designed by a whitewater park design firm.

"It's like a section of rapids that could exist in West Virginia or Colorado," Gary Hunter, a member of the Northern Michigan Paddling Club, told me a couple of years after it opened. "If you're into paddling rapids, it's the only true whitewater course currently in northern Lower Michigan."

The lower section is designed for walking, easily allowing a paddler to carry their kayak back upstream to run that section over and over. The farther up you go, the larger the drops and rapids. For those new to the sport, it allows you to run the easier, lower rapids, several times before tackling the harder upstream sections. May and early June are the best times for river flow.

But it's not the place to try an aluminum canoe: You need a true, whitewater kayak with a neoprene skirt to stay dry. Another option, if you just want to give it a try, is to rent a Ducky from local outfitter Bahnhof Sports in Petoskey. Duckys are 1- and 2-person inflatable kayaks. They are pretty stable, with the ability to bounce off rocks and boulders. Weighing a little over 20 pounds, they're easy to carry upstream for multiple runs, and easy to exit in case of a tip-over and at take-out.

For hikers and bikers, the recreation area offers a 1.5-mile combination of paved and unpaved trails from River Bend Park up to Lake Street—and you can see little of the city. It remains pristine along the floor of the river gorge.

For years, the Bear River's natural beauty was obscured by industry and dams altering the flow of the river. In the early 2000s, residents started cleaning up the site and dams were removed, restoring the natural river flow. The Bear River Valley Recreation Area today offers lots of activities and a beautiful natural area for all seasons.

Terrell's Trail Notes

T A wide, paved trail that passes a couple of picnic shelters runs from the park on Lake Street—which is the north end of the recreation area—south to Sheridan Street. The half mile from Sheridan Street to River Bend Park is a natural trail offering some of the best upper river views.

T The North Country Trail (NCT)—which runs from the New York/Vermont border to North Dakota—also blazes a path through the park. Follow the blue paint marks on trees and signs. It's a scenic, mostly natural trail with great valley and river views. The paved trail doesn't always offer the best river views. Just north of the West Side Shelter is where the NCT leads off the paved path and crosses the river on a footbridge. Continue straight ahead along the gravel path on the west side of the river and don't cross the footbridge. This is where you get your best whitewater views. The gravel path rejoins the paved pathway and continues to offer river views. You pass Mitchell Street and enter Mineral Well Park before reaching the Lake Street Bridge. The NCT continues along the east side of the river once it crosses the footbridge and joins Little Traverse Wheelway in a little over a half mile.

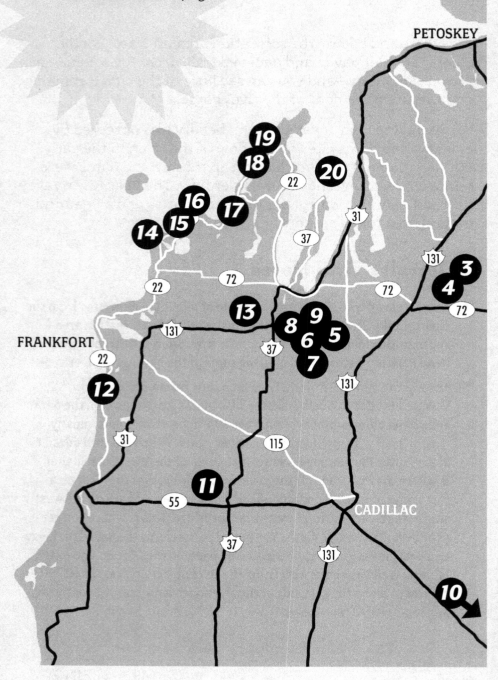

See also
Coastal Sunsets, *page 53*

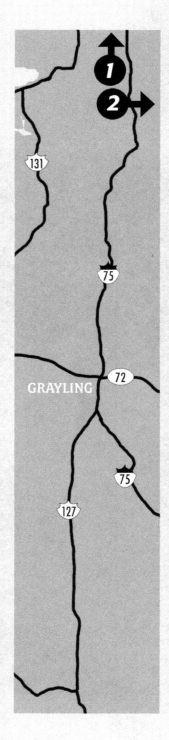

Summer

Coastal summer sunsets can make your day

If there's one thing we shouldn't take for granted, it's a sunset. It can be a mood changer when you catch a particularly beautiful sunset, and living up here it can happen quite often, particularly along the Lake Michigan coastline during summer.

There are few things in life—at least for me—that can match a spectacular sunset along the coast. It can linger with our long daylight hours, morphing into a kaleidoscope of colors as the sun drops, like an ever changing palette. Sunsets have actually been proven to help fight stress, depression, and anxiety.

Having a rough day? Head to the coast and let a summer sunset wash your worries away.

Empire Bluff

There is one spot along the Sleeping Bear Dunes National Lakeshore that is my favorite for a number of reasons: Empire Bluff Trail. Rising over 400 feet above lake level, it offers some of the best views of the lake and shoreline. From that lofty perch, views stretch north to the Manitou Islands and the Sleeping Bear Dunes, as well as to the south, around Platte Bay, at a distance of over 25 miles. With a beautiful sunset, it's a place to sit, linger, meditate, and enjoy one of Mother Nature's most spectacular shows.

The other reason I like the Empire Bluff Trail is that you can't drive up and walk a short distance to enjoy the stunning views. It's not a long hike—only 1.5 miles round trip on the out-and-back trail—but you do have to climb a couple of hills to get there. That limits the number of people willing to make the trek and makes it much more enjoyable for those who do. If you drive up to the overlook on Pierce Stocking Scenic Drive to catch a sunset, you often find hordes of people stretched out on blankets and occupying the benches.

Once you get out on Empire Bluff, there are benches where you may find a few people sitting. I've even seen some putting up hammocks in trees along the bluff to really relax and enjoy the sunset. The crowd is never very large. You do have to be back down to the trailhead parking lot by 10 p.m., although it probably still won't be dark.

Terrell's Trail Notes

🚩 The trailhead parking lot is partway up the bluff, off Wilco Road, just south of the village of Empire. There are 6 interpretive signs along the trail that point out historical and geological features of the trail and area.

🚩 The trail immediately begins a moderate climb from the parking lot through a forest. It's the longest climb along the trail before it levels out and descends into an upland meadow. There's a bench along this portion of trail that offers some nice overlooks of Empire and North Bar Lake.

🚩 The trail has a couple more short climbs before you emerge from the forest along the edge of the bluff. A boardwalk takes you out along the bluff to an area with benches offering magnificent views of all there is to see. Gulls will be flying about eye level along the coast, and sometimes you can see people far below looking like ants scurrying along the beach. South Manitou Island floats on a blue horizon. It's one of the best views in Lower Michigan in my opinion—one you will want to linger and enjoy as the sun slowly drops below the lake.

🚩 Don't forget your camera and a flashlight for the walk back down through the darkening woods as dusk settles. This is one hike I've been doing now for nearly 40 years and never tire of doing it again.

1

Ocqueoc River

the Lower Peninsula's only named waterfall

Approaching the Ocqueoc River crossing on M-68, halfway between Onoway and Rogers City, my friend stopped talking and listened.

"It sounds like a waterfall," he said, not believing what he was hearing. "I didn't know we had any waterfalls in the Lower Peninsula, thought they were all in the UP."

He's not alone. The Upper Peninsula is home to over 200 named falls and countless unnamed ones. Our peninsula, on the other hand, has only one recognized waterfall, the Ocqueoc Falls.

It's a hidden gem, according to Ron Olson, chief of the DNR's Recreation Division. Ocqueoc is an Ojibway word meaning "sacred."

Unlike many waterfalls in the UP, where you have to be content to just stand alongside and gaze at their beauty, Ocqueoc invites you right in. "With four small rapids and a pool of cool water just perfect for splashing around in, people just feel that urge to get in the water and enjoy it," he elaborated.

Walking down to the waterfalls, we could hear the laughter and shouts of children cavorting and playing in the river and the falls and jumping into the pools created below the cascades. The cool waters did look tempting on a hot August afternoon.

One of the mothers watching the children remarked that a waterfall brings out the child in all of us, as she sat dangling her legs in the river.

"I never get tired of coming here when we are up visiting family. It's a beautiful spot, never crowded, and the kids absolutely love it. It's not well known. People downstate tell me, when I mention a waterfall in Lower Michigan, that I must mean the UP," laughed the Grand Rapids mother.

The area received a makeover in 2012. A barrier-free, paved trail from the parking lot to the waterfalls and two picnic areas surfaced with crushed limestone were added. Access to the river is now provided by either a ramp or a rock climb.

"Our biggest challenge was making the bluff, the historical route to the river, accessible," pointed out Brenda Curtis, DNR forest recreation planner. "We wanted this facility to be family-friendly and considered all details. Three routes of various challenge levels were created. Now everyone can experience the rock climb and have a choice on how to get to the river, and, with platform transfers top and bottom, even those in a wheelchair."

Terrell's Trail Notes

T There's also the Ocqueoc Falls Bicentennial Pathway, a state forest hiking trail that's divided into four loops and a small state forest campground. The waterfall is the primary thing that most visitors come to see, but don't ignore the 6-mile scenic trail, which is also open to mountain biking, according to Curtis.

T The trail begins by passing through a red pine plantation, then ascends a ridge that looks down on the river snaking through a valley flanked by towering wooded ridges. The return trail offers a scenic streamside hike.

T The rustic, state forest campground, across the road from the trailhead, is small; offering only 14 sites, but most are located along the edge of a scenic ridge overlooking the river.

"It's the kind of place that if you stumble across it, you immediately feel like you've hit the vacation jackpot," mused Olson.

T Visitors need the Recreation Passport, required by the state, to enter the park.

The megaphone in the woods.

2

Agnes S. Andreae Nature Preserve

**shush!
it's forest listening time**

A "nature megaphone," big enough to sit in, is being discovered in northern Michigan. It's believed to be the only one in North America.

Located in the Agnes S. Andreae Nature Preserve, just east of I-75 near Indian River and part of the Little Traverse Conservancy, it was erected here in 2019. The idea came from conservancy staff member Charles Dawley, who saw it online. A Petoskey High School Building Trades class constructed it. Nature megaphones first appeared in Europe in Estonia.

This takes "forest bathing" to a whole new level.

It is a bit of a drive, around 90 miles, which I found worth it to view this incredible structure and hike the trails in the Andreae Nature Preserve and the adjoining Boyd Banwell Nature Preserve. The trails, mostly easy hiking, offer about 5 miles between the two preserves, with many scenic overlooks of the swift-flowing Pigeon River. It's one of Michigan's Wild Scenic Rivers, and views from trails along high banks definitely support the designation.

"We've been very pleased with the addition of the megaphone and the interest created in both it and the conservancy," said Kieran Fleming, conservancy director. "We placed it in a destination that requires a little bit of hiking to get to. We wanted people to experience the beauty of the preserves as well."

It's about a mile hike back to the megaphone from any of three trailheads you can start from. The structure is nestled into a picturesque wooded ridge overlooking an open valley below and forested hills on the far side.

The idea behind the design is that it amplifies sounds filtering into the large opening, allowing you to concentrate on listening. You climb into the structure, sit quietly, and listen. I could clearly hear leaves rustling around the structure, which I assumed to be little critters moving around after I disappeared in the cone. It amplified songbirds chirping.

"Early morning and early evening hours are the best time to visit for more bird and wildlife activity. It's also best to visit on a light-wind day," Fleming added.

If the uniqueness doesn't intrigue you to visit, remember it's believed to be the only "nature megaphone" in North America. That, and hiking along one of northern Michigan's wild, unspoiled rivers, was reason enough for me.

Terrell's Trail Notes

🚩 Figuring the experience would be best enjoyed individually, I visited on a weekday in early June and had it all to myself. I chose the easternmost trailhead, which is just north of Afton, off M-68. About 6 miles east of I-75, turn north on Quarry Road. In half a mile turn west on Dunn Road, and travel another half mile to the preserve trailhead marked by a sign. The trail begins beyond the locked gate in the parking area. I passed only a mother and daughter, headed back from the megaphone as I hiked out.

🚩 You begin at signpost 20, a mile from the megaphone, which is near signpost 12. I chose to take a longer route to get more river views along the hike. I went to post 21 and over to posts 14 through 13, which was around 2.5 miles. There were a couple of nice river views from high bluffs south of post 17 and 13—quick out-and-back hikes.

🚩 When you approach the 10-foot-long audio device nestled among the trees overlooking the valley, you can't help but feel awe. The beautifully handcrafted structure, made of polished, treated lumber, took my breath away and I just stared at it for a good minute. Crawling inside and forest-listening was the "icing on the cake."

🚩 After experiencing the phone, it's just a short hike to a bench overlooking a panoramic view of a horseshoe bend in the river and the lush, green valley stretching out below you—another place to just sit and enjoy an incredible vista. From there, it's about a mile over to the historic Andreae stone cabin, located on the river, and a footbridge crossing the river to the cabin. Along the way, you pass a couple of scenic sites: one on the river and another overlook from a high bluff. From there it's a 1.5-mile return along the upper trails to the trailhead parking area on Dunn Road.

3

Upper Manistee Headwaters Preserve

a northern Michigan gem

The new Upper Manistee Headwaters Preserve in Kalkaska County is the essence of northern Michigan.

What struck me was the beauty of the pristine, blue lake surrounded by an equally pristine forest. Wetlands are interspersed between as you proceed around the lake, which is often in view. The blending of blue waters, green forest, and a blue sky dotted with fleecy white clouds reflected in the lake was "pure" northern Michigan.

This large, 1,288-acre parcel of land—the former Boy Scout Camp Tapico—surrounds spring-fed Grass Lake with a mixture of forests, open meadows, kettle-hole ponds, wetlands, and even a mile of the north branch of the Manistee River. The fact that the property has a near-complete lack of invasive species makes it truly "pure" northern Michigan. It's extremely valuable as a public preserve because of the quality of native vegetation, according to the Grand Traverse Regional Land Conservancy (GTRLC).

There are around 6 miles of trails available for hiking, biking, snowshoeing, and cross country skiing in winter, ranging from old two-tracks, forest roads, and new trails. The terrain is very flat for easy hiking.

At the south end of the lake, there's a bench to enjoy the full-length lake view, a restroom, a fishing dock, and an amphitheater where they hold occasional programs.

On the east side of the lake, a two-track offering more lake views leads to a couple of scenic spots with benches, a picnic shelter with multiple tables, and a restroom. On the west side of the lake, they have built a nice, graveled walkway through wetlands that leads to more stunning bench views. It's about a 2-mile round-trip trek up either side of Grass Lake.

I hiked back along the east side of the lake to a bench with a "jaw-dropping" view. I watched fleecy clouds float over while my goldendoodle, Lulu, cavorted in the lake, chasing sticks. She was on a leash as we hiked.

It just doesn't get much better than this.

Kudos to GTRLC for their valiant effort in saving this sprawling piece of land from sure development. The herculean effort took four years and donations of nearly four million dollars to insure keeping it available as public domain and out of developers' hands.

Terrell's Trail Notes

T From Traverse City, head through Kalkaska on SR 612 to the four-way stop. Continue straight through the stop. The road becomes Grass Lake Road, which turns to dirt after a couple of miles. A large sign heralds your arrival at the Headwaters Preserve.

T Park and proceed around the gate. Follow the half-mile drive to the south end of Grass Lake—or you can follow a trail that parallels the drive on the east side. It's half a mile either way. A trail to the west of the drive is a meandering mile to the lake.

T There are posted signs with numbers corresponding to the map which you can download at www.GTRLC.org. Follow the two-track around the east side to signpost 3. You can also follow the trail, but it doesn't offer any lake views until you get past signpost 4. It's about 1.5 miles either way from the parking area. From signpost 4, head left and in about .3 miles you will come to a split in the trail. Either way, it's a short distance to two lovely spots on the lake where you can sit and enjoy the splendid views. It's a mile-long loop from post 4 if you proceed straight ahead. An interesting posting at the north end of the lake along the loop describes the Lost Compass Swamp. You wonder how it got that name.

T From the south end, head over to signpost 5, along the west side of the lake, where you can follow a combination of dirt and gravel pathways through forest and wetlands, offering a couple more scenic bench views.

T They ask that you don't haul in any watercraft, contain your bait, and pack out whatever you bring in to prevent invasive species entering the system. Swimming and wading is permitted, but no lifeguards are on duty. The area is open dawn to dusk.

4

Manistee River

small stream paddling

You tend to think of the Manistee, one of Michigan's longest rivers at 163 miles, as a wide, stodgy river that plods along its journey to Lake Michigan. That's the part most of us see in our travels across northern Michigan.

From M-72 on over to the lake, the river averages between 60 and 100 feet across, and it does offer scenic floats beneath towering bluffs. But, it doesn't have the intimate feel of many of our smaller, faster-flowing streams.

Head above M-72 for a float on the upper Manistee, where the width ranges between 30 and 45 feet, and cottages are less frequent to non-existent. It feels comfortable and less intimidating.

You can start your float from three different spots. The old, lumbering "ghost town" of Deward is about a 6- to 7-hour, 18-mile float down to M-72; from Cameron Bridge Road, it's a 14-mile, 5-hour float; and from the CR 612 bridge, it's a 10-mile, 3-hour float.

Deward is the most difficult put-in to reach. You have to follow Manistee River Road—a rough dirt road—for 5 or 6 miles above CR 612 before turning down a two-track marked by a "binocular" sign to a sandy parking area. Then, you must carry your kayak or canoe a quarter mile to the put-in. A cart is useful, and so is four-wheel drive to get there.

The other two put-ins—Cameron Road and CR 612 at paved bridge crossings—are much easier to reach. Normally, when I've kayaked from Deward, it's down to the CR 612 Bridge, which is about an 8-mile float. Friends spot cars for a nice leisurely outing. It makes a long day if you float all the way down to M-72.

The upper river is clear, meandering, and beautiful. The depth averages between one and three feet. The bottom is mostly gravel, which makes it an excellent trout stream. You most likely will come across fishers wading the river. Just make sure they know you are there and stay wide. It's all friendly and there's plenty of room.

This was the heart of the last great stand of virgin white pine in the late 1800s, thus the birth of Deward, which died when the last logs floated down the river. You can still see weathered stumps dotting surrounding hills and meadows as you float down the river.

A few cabins are interspersed among large holdings of public land, which lends to the intimate seclusion you feel paddling this section of river. It flows through grasslands, and is often divided into channels winding through numerous little grass islands. There are a few giant white pines along the river that the lumberman's ax missed. If you paddle upstream a short distance from Deward, you will find beaver dams. This section of the river gets as narrow as 30 feet at times. Because of its remoteness, it's a great place to spot deer, waterfowl, and eagles perched high in trees.

You'll see few paddlers north of the CR 612 Bridge because it's a longer trip back to popular Shel Haven Canoe and Kayak Rental located on the north side of M-72. The livery trip from CR 612 and back is their most popular. Summer days, especially weekends, can be busy on that section of river. The largest crowds are encountered from mid-June through Labor Day.

Most of the paddlers and tubers tend to follow the main section of river, but the river often divides into channels as it winds around all the little grass islands. I love to play around and follow some of the side channels. Sometimes you get through, sometimes not. Occasionally I come across a downed tree and have to go back, but that's the fun of exploring—and, it gets you away from the maddening crowd.

Better yet, grab some friends to spot cars and head up to Deward.

5

Greilick Outdoor

a treat to explore

Here's a wonderful, wild space to explore, with hiking, mountain biking, and cross country skiing and snowshoeing in the winter. That's just the start of the appeal of the Greilick Outdoor Recreation & Education Center, which is owned by Traverse City's Rotary Club.

A Boy Scout camp for years—the 500-acre property now known as GO REC is open for daily outdoor use by area residents. There are bears, bobcats, foxes, coyotes, and plenty of deer to spot on hikes.

Right now it's open to visitors for day use only. Eventually, it will be open for camping and cabin rentals for family fun and adventure.

The outdoor potential is great. The 500 acres include frontage on three lakes—including Rennie Lake—and is managed for wildlife habitat as part of the Grand Traverse Regional Land Conservancy. There are numerous trails and old two-tracks that head out into the acreage, offering miles of exploring. You can also connect with the Brown Bridge Quiet Area, the Boardman River Trail, North Country Trail, and Muncie Lakes Pathway. There are geocaching locations scattered around the property. During winter, they plan on grooming a couple of miles for cross country skiing.

This is my new favorite getaway spot. I head out into the acreage for miles of hiking and never see anybody. It's beautiful, peaceful, and soul satisfying. Get out and explore this scenic piece of property on foot or by mountain bike. You'll wonder where you are at times—but who cares? Enjoy the experience and scenery of this diverse countryside. You'll eventually come out somewhere recognizable. Another plus is that it is all marked "no hunting."

Terrell's Trail Notes

T From the parking lot, which is located off Hobbs Highway, head through the gate. The paved road quickly turns to dirt. Go right by the store building at the intersection, and the two-track heads out into the hinterland for a little over a mile before reaching the wells on the south side of the property; the blue and red trails intersect and cross it at various times.

T To reach the beginning of the red trail, head up a two-track leading off the main road at a sign marked "cottages." Follow it past cottages and an amphitheater. The trail begins with a red blaze on a tree by the disc golf course. In roughly 2 miles, you cross Ranch Rudolf Road, and the red trail soon joins the Boardman River Trail (BRT). A right on the BRT will get you quickly into Brown Bridge Quiet Area. Go left, and in about .75 miles, the red trail again heads left, crossing back over Ranch Rudolf Road and eventually joining blue trail spurs.

T When you are using the trails, they ask that you register at the trailhead by signing on to an app with your smartphone. If you don't have a smartphone, you can go online and register before heading to the trailhead.

When this second footbridge was installed in 2019 over
the Boardman River in the Brown Bridge Quiet Area,
it completed a 5-mile loop trail along the river.

6

Brown Bridge Quiet Area

trail now complete

The Brown Bridge Quiet Area, one of the most popular outdoor venues in our region, improved dramatically in 2019 when a second footbridge was placed across the Boardman River near the site of the old dam's power house. Now, with the first bridge put in two years earlier—about 2.5 miles upstream as the crow flies—you can complete a loop along the river. Prior to that, you had a choice of hiking along one side of the river or the other, but with the removal of the old dam and restoration of the river valley, it made sense to add the footbridges.

The quiet area is appealing in many different ways, and one is that it's not far from Traverse City. The City actually owns the area, which it purchased nearly a century ago when the river was dammed. It has always been a popular spot for hikers—especially along the bluffs—but really blossomed in the 1980s when the City erected barriers to keep out off-road vehicles and horseback traffic; made trails by adding boardwalks, overlooks, and bridges where necessary; and, most importantly, made it a quiet area. No camping, no motorized activity, no horses, no mountain bikes; just hiking, snowshoeing, and skiing are welcomed activities. It's popular in all seasons.

There are around 7 miles of trails, with the loop trail being a little over 5 miles to complete. I find the quiet area enticing because of its hiking diversity. You meander through hardwood forests of beautiful old trees—especially white and red pine, many being well over a century old. At times I feel like I'm walking through an old-growth forest. There's little undergrowth because the large, old trees block most of the sunlight. It's almost a reverent feeling.

Other times, you hike on high bluffs above the river valley where you can gaze down on the river snaking along the lowlands through breaks in the forested ridge. A couple of platform overlooks along the ridge offer stunning vistas. Occasionally, you can see eagles floating above the valley, probably looking for game. Deer are often spotted along the river.

The trails amble through scenic upland and lowland forests, and always, that dazzling, Blue Ribbon trout stream is nearby. Boardman River is considered one of Michigan's top ten trout streams, and I consider this one of the top ten hikes around Traverse City.

Terrell's Trail Notes

🚩 I like to start the loop hike at signpost 1, which is located near the kayak/canoe site off Brown Bridge Road. There are picnic tables at the site and an outhouse nearby. The trail heads into the forest and meanders along ridges for about 1.5 miles before reaching post 2. Once you leave the trailhead, you won't see much of the river—except for an occasional glimpse—until you reach the Grasshopper Creek loop and bridge crossing at post 5.

🚩 At post 3, you have a choice. The Grasshopper loop is about a mile around to the bridge with some nice river views. Or, you can head down the ridge from post 3, reaching the bridge and post 5 in about .2 miles, shortening the total hike. I like the longer version.

🚩 Heading south from the bridge, the next .7 miles along the Boardman offers many river views. When you reach the section of trail along a 900-foot boardwalk, you have another choice. Take the boardwalk or continue to follow the trail along the river as it enters the broad, open valley that used to house Brown Bridge Pond.

🚩 The boardwalk leads to a long, steep set of stairs to the top of the ridge. You can hike along that for about a mile and a half, and there are a couple of jaw-dropping overlooks before you head off the ridge to post 12. It's a quick hike across the old earthen dam to reach the new bridge and complete the loop hike. The numbered signposts follow the ridge trail.

🚩 I prefer to start out into the valley instead of taking the boardwalk after post 5. You follow trails and an old two-track underneath the ridge. The river at times swings away from you, crossing the valley and back again. In a couple of miles, you reach the old earthen dam. The trail crossing the earthen dam offers some splendid views looking up the valley.

🚩 The loop hike falls between 5.5 and a little over 6 miles, depending on the route you choose. Whichever way you choose to complete the loop hike, they are all scenic and enjoyable.

7

East Creek Reserve

short, scenic trails

If you're looking for a short, scenic hike that offers a good workout and beautiful views of a deep, wooded ravine with a creek rushing through it, then East Creek Reserve is the hike for you.

Haven't heard of it? You're not alone. It's a lightly used trail system that is a little off the radar. It's located along a rough seasonal county road that serves as a snowmobile trail in the winter.

Think of it as an undiscovered gem that's well worth the drive and trek and likely devoid of crowds. You'll probably have it to yourself, so linger and enjoy the views along this scenic trail.

The trail system is tucked into the Pere Marquette State Forest, south of the Boardman River and east of Garfield Road.
The trailhead I prefer is on Mayfield Road, which turns into a seasonal road. It's about a mile east of Garfield Road.
There is also a trailhead on Wadsworth Road, also seasonal. Both the Boardman River Trail and Shore-to-Shore Horseback Trail pass briefly through the system. The horseback trail that can devastate hiking is all on Mayfield Road. The Boardman River Trail follows a portion of the East Creek trail.

The system is divided into two loops—the north side of Mayfield Road and the south side. The two loops are tied together by out-and-back trails and the road.

This is a rugged corner of the state forest. The East Creek trail climbs and follows a ridge that borders the creek rushing through the deep ravine almost 150 feet below. The Brown Bridge Quiet Area with the Boardman River and miles of trails along tall ridges bordering the river valley is less than a mile to the north on the Boardman River Trail. A few miles east, the North Country Trail passes through the Valley of the Giants.

East Creek Reserve is owned by Rotary Charities and managed as part of the Grand Traverse Conservation District.
The 560-acre reserve offers almost 4 miles of trails, and the Conservation District lists the difficulty level as easy. I think that's off. There's a .3-mile connector trail for the northern loop that's a bit of a thigh-burner, and another steep climb on the south loop. It's not problematic if you take your time and enjoy the view—especially along the north loop connector—but I wouldn't rate it easy.

On the climb from the Mayfield Road trailhead, you can see East Creek rushing along the deep valley until it disappears. Looking through trees along the ridge, you occasionally catch glimpses of ridges on the other side of the chasm. It reminds me of hikes that I've taken along forest streams in the Appalachian Mountains on the Blue Ridge Parkway.

This is a pretty hike in the spring, summer, and fall, but impossible to reach in winter. It's not a long hike, but will still provide a workout. It's also a good Fido hike: they can jump into the creek for a quick cool-down.

Terrell's Trail Notes

T The Mayfield Road trailhead sits almost in the middle of the two loops.

T From the trailhead—which has pretty views of East Creek—the trail begins to climb almost immediately, heading up the tall ridge and topping out about 150 feet above the valley. Fortunately, the trail climbs diagonally, instead of straight up, before reaching the first intersection on top at .3 miles. The trail is marked with yellow triangles. Head east as it passes a gas well and loops north to intersect the out-and-back trail from the Wadsworth Road trailhead. Continuing across an open meadow, you pass another trail intersection before reaching the marker where the Boardman River Trail passes through on its way to Brown Bridge.

T The East Creek trail meanders south a half a mile along the ridge, affording great valley views before eventually descending the spur you initially climbed. For the south trail, you have to hike a quarter mile west along Mayfield Road before the trail heads back over to East Creek—a very pretty section along the stream the dogs will love. After another half mile, the trail crosses back over Mayfield Road and climbs another ridge, meandering along it before descending and returning to the trailhead in about 1.5 miles.

T Hiking around the north loop is about 1.5 miles, and the south loop adds another 2.2 miles.

8

Sand Lakes Quiet Area

an oasis for hiking and skiing

One of my favorite places for a quick getaway is Sand Lakes Quiet Area. The name says it all: It's a world away from the bustle and noise of everyday life. I take off down the trail and feel the stress and complexities of the plugged-in world melt away as I'm immersed in the silence of the surrounding forest, hills, and small lakes that make up this 2,800-acre tract. It was designated a nonmotorized "quiet area" in 1973.

The 6-mile perimeter trail passes five small, beautiful blue lakes as it snakes across rolling hills through an oak and pine forest, making a complete circle. It's only a couple of miles down, around the first couple of lakes and back up, if you want a quick, scenic hike. It's also a popular camping spot, which is allowed throughout the quiet area.

Most day-trippers enter the area from the Broomhead Road trailhead. Most campers enter from the Sand Lakes Road trailhead. Both offer adequate parking areas. It's slightly under a mile on a spur trail from Broomhead to connect with the main trail, and about a half mile from Sand Lakes Road. Round trip for the long circle loop from Broomhead is 8 miles, and from Sand Lakes Road less than 7 miles. Weekends around the first couple of lakes—because they are easy to get to—can be crowded with campers during the summer. The east end of the quiet area is anchored by popular Guernsey Lake State Forest Campground with 30 sites. It is not on the main 6-mile pathway, but has easy spurs that connect with it.

Don't be surprised if you see whitetail deer while hiking. Black bears have been spotted occasionally, but not often. The area is popular for hunting as well. Avoid it during the firearms deer hunting season from November 15 to 30.

The trails are well marked and signed, but it's still a good idea to have a map with you. Old forest roads and fire lanes crisscross the area, which can be a bit confusing at times. The North Country Trail, that goes from New York to North Dakota through Michigan, also joins the Sand Lakes trail for a bit.

Sand Lakes has all that you could want for a quick day hike or overnight campout. There are small, scenic lakes—and best of all, great trails for hiking and mountain biking. This is a popular trail system for cross country skiers and snowshoers in the winter. After the trees are cloaked in a mantle of fresh fallen snow, it's like skiing through a snow globe.

Terrell's Trail Notes

T Leaving Broomhead Road, follow the signposts from 1 to 3, where the trail joins the 6-mile loop that circles the quiet area. If you're coming from Sand Lakes Road, it's a quick half mile down to join the loop trail just above the first lake at post 5. There's a privy for campers and trail users. Don't bypass seeing this first lake, which I think is the most beautiful of the many small lakes you pass. It can be mesmerizing when the sun shines. The Caribbean-like blue of the small, glacially created lake is stunning.

T If you want just a 2- or 3-mile hike, continue on around the lakeshore where an unnamed trail leads over to a second lake with a cathedral-like area of tall red pines. From there, a trail leads around the right side of the lake to a third small lake. The main trail sits just above that third lake, and heads back to signposts 3 and 5.

T If you want to hike the loop, follow the marked posts from 5 through 16. You will pass more small lakes with benches positioned at scenic locations along the path. I particularly like the small Pit Lake on the backside of the trail system, where I've seen deer a few times while enjoying the view. At post 12, you'll find a spur trail leading over to Guernsey Lake Campground.

T From signpost 16, head north through post 4 and you'll find the spur trails leading back up to the trailhead parking areas.

9

Valley of the Giants

a hike through the Valley of the Giants is almost Tolkien-like, always peaceful and beautiful, the 200-year-old trees making you think of Middle-earth

It's easy to fantasize as you walk along this portion of the North Country Trail (NCT), underneath this colossal canopy of white and red pine, cedars, and oak trees, stretching high above you. Many are believed to be 150 to over 200 years old. It's easy to feel dwarfed by both time and the trees.

When many were just seedlings, the War of 1812 was just ending, and a couple of other historical battles—the Battle of Waterloo and the Battle of New Orleans—had just taken place.

Once you reach the valley floor, much of the trail follows scenic 22 Creek, a swift-flowing, babbling tributary to the Boardman River. The creek flows through a deep valley, which is probably what helped preserve all of the old giants from the lumberman's ax. It would have been difficult to transport the downed trees out of that valley.

The valley can be reached from a couple of different points along the NCT. Both Scharmen and Mayfield roads, just east of the Boardman River, offer access. The trail runs between the two roads, and a trek involves an out-and-back from both locations, or spotting a car at one end.

Either way, the scenic trail skirts many ancient giants and provides a good workout as you climb out of the valley. You pass a rather large beaver impoundment on 22 Creek; there's a lodge and well-constructed dam. I marvel at these furry little engineers every time I pass it.

It always seems cooler down in the valley along the creek during the heat of summer, and fall offers scenic colors and nice overlooks of the valley.

I've seen deer and black bears in the valley, and foxes along the ridge above the valley. I haven't seen a beaver yet, but I've heard their tails slapping the water, warning my dog and me that they were nearby.

Photo: Adobe Stock

The Trailheads

Follow Scharmen Road—off Brown Bridge Road—for a little over 4 miles until it swings right and becomes Hodge Road. The NCT crosses the road at this point. There is plenty of room for parking.

Mayfield Road heads east off Garfield Road / CO 611 as you head towards Mayfield. It's about 6 miles to where the NCT crosses the road. The trail is on a two-track. Head north on the two-track for about .2 miles until the NCT swings away. You park here and hike north along the trail.

Neither dirt road is in great shape. It's slow going, but worth the inconvenience once you experience this hike.

Terrell's Trail Notes

🇹 From Scharmen Road, follow the NCT as it heads up the hill. In a little over .3 miles, you cross a two-track along the top of a ridge. Follow the NCT as it proceeds off the ridge, down into the valley. Once you reach the valley floor, it's a short distance to a wooden sign stretched above the trail proclaiming it the Valley of the Giants.

🇹 From this point on, you are among the large, old trees. When you reach 22 Creek, the trail follows it for about a mile. You will come across a bench along the creek, a beautiful resting spot. The trail crosses the creek ahead, and then it's about a mile to the beaver impoundment.

🇹 From the parking area north of Mayfield Road, follow the NCT about a half a mile to where it heads down into the valley. A picturesque wooden bridge crossing 22 Creek appears in another half mile, and not long after that, you start walking among the giants heading up the valley. After a mile you come to the beaver impoundment.

🇹 The beaver lodge sits along the shore, and past that, you come to the large dam stretching across the creek, effectively creating the good-sized pond. Enough water escapes through the dam, though, that the creek doesn't seem to lose any volume as it flows on down the valley to the Boardman River.

🇹 It's roughly 2 miles from the beaver pond to either of the two parking places to begin the trail, or a trek of 4 miles from one road to the other, if spotting a car.

10

Red Hill Lookout

a rugged climb to a big vista

I've always enjoyed hiking the North Country Trail (NCT) throughout our region as it winds north along the Manistee River, continues through the Jordan River valley, climbing to the Skyline Trail above Petoskey, and follows the Bear River valley through Petoskey. The views along the many miles of trail throughout northwestern Lower Michigan are considered some of the finest within the 1,100 miles of NCT in the Wolverine State.

Backpackers on the North Country Trail approach Red Hill Lookout.

Among the numerous "eye-candy" views you come across hiking the North Country Trail high ridges, one of my favorite vistas is the Red Hill Lookout, high above the Manistee River valley. It offers a sweeping bird's-eye view of the Tippy Dam Pond reservoir and river valley stretching for 20 or so miles to the tall hills on the other side. It's enticing throughout the summer, but a beautiful, sunny fall day can enhance the vista.

One of the things that I like about this location is that it's kind of obscure and not as well known as other overlooks in our region that often draw large crowds, like Highbanks Rollway, Jordan River Valley overlook, the Skyline Trail, and Bear River valley. The lack of a crowd has as much to do with the effort required to get to this viewing point as anything else.

Unlike Rollway and Jordan River Valley overlooks, you can't drive to within a 100 feet of this viewing point. Even the Skyline Trail, that necessitates some hiking, requires nowhere near the same effort to get up to Red Hill Lookout. That means once I do get up there, I can stretch out, relax under a shade tree, and not worry about being trampled by others wanting to get a selfie looking out over the valley. What you see more of here are backpackers. The 20-mile loop formed by the NCT and Manistee River Trail on the other side of the river valley, is one the most popular backpacking routes in the Lower Peninsula.

The best trailhead to use is the Upper Manistee trailhead, located off Coates Highway just west of Red Bridge. It's a trailhead for both trails: a spur trail joins the NCT along the west side of the river and the Manistee River Trail heads north along the east side of the river. It's a little over 1.5 miles from the trailhead up to Red Hill Lookout, or a round trip of about .75 miles. The rugged climb is over 350 feet of elevation change one way. You end up at a little over 1,100 feet above sea level once you reach Red Hill, which is near the location of an old fire tower from the 1920s.

Pick a nice day, pack a lunch, a camera, binoculars, and enjoy the view.

Terrell's Trail Notes

🅣 The parking area—marked with a sign—is on the north side of Coates Highway, shortly after crossing Red Bridge heading west. Signs and maps are posted at the trailhead.

🅣 From the parking area, a trail quickly leads to a split, where the Manistee River Trail heads one way and a marked spur heads up to intersect the NCT. It's a steep climb up a ridge to join the multistate trail that winds 4,600 miles from the New York/Vermont border, through the Wolverine State, on to the middle of North Dakota. Once you intersect the NCT, you continue to climb—not as steeply—and you start to get peeks down into the valley through the trees. You only occasionally get a glimpse of the river because it's so far below.

🅣 Eventually, as the trail starts to level off, you'll intersect a junction with a sign posted "Red Hill Lookout." It's about 100 yards up; a short quick climb. The area between the sign and the lookout is often used by backpackers for camping. It makes a great spot with an outstanding view only steps away. The spot where the old fire tower stood is about a quarter of a mile up the trail and marked by old footings. There really isn't a distant view from this location, but the old tower, during its heyday, would have been high enough to look out over the forest for great distances.

11

Lost Lake Pathway

nesting loons and bald eagles

When I want a leisurely hike along lakes and river, the Lost Lake Pathway routinely comes to mind. It is an easy-paced pathway for hikers that runs along Lake Dubonet and the beginnings of the Platte River.

About a mile of the trail hugs the Lake Dubonet shoreline, and the remaining 5.5-mile pathway meanders through a landscape of transitional small sinkhole lakes created by glacial debris and melting ice deposits—a microcosm of our regional topography.

Lake Dubonet itself was created in 1956, when a stream—the headwaters for the Platte River—was dammed to improve fishing and wildlife habitat; both goals were successfully accomplished. The pathway passes over the earthen dam, and the popular fishing lake is now home to nesting loons and bald eagles.

The trail passes a couple of large bogs along the back section as it goes around the Lost Lake basin. The small lake at the north end of the basin is all that remains. In just a couple of centuries, it will probably completely disappear. Such is the fate of small pit lakes created by the last glacier passing through here 11,000 years ago.

At times, the trail follows century-old railroad beds created during the logging era. Some of the beautiful red pine stands that you pass through are considered that old; they were probably seedlings at the end of that era.

When I first moved here in 1979, the pathway had interpretive markers placed along the trail explaining the history, topography, and nature of the area, but they're now long gone. Unfortunately, the DNR, in cost cutting moves, didn't replace them as they deteriorated. There are maps and post markers at most trail intersections, and the well-worn pathway is fairly easy to follow, but you do have to pay attention as forest roads and other trails crisscross the area and pathway.

The Shore-to-Shore Horseback Trail also passes through here, crossing the Lost Lake Pathway at least a couple of times. There was a time in the early 1990s when horseback riding on the trail was a problem. Today, thanks to signs, education, and Traverse City DNR Field Office follow-through, riders follow the rules.

A state forest campground overlooking Lake Dubonet is located along the first loop. The 50-site rustic campground includes a boat launch.

Terrell's Trail Notes

🇹 The pathway is divided into loops—which is nice for hiking, depending on how much terrain you want to cover. The entire pathway is around 6.5 miles, and is also popular with mountain bikers. Although it's an easy pathway, I've been hiking, mountain biking, and skiing it for over 40 years and have never tired of it. Wildlife sightings are normal here, which keeps it interesting.

🇹 The trailhead for the pathway is at the end of Wildwood Road, which exits U.S. 31 just past Interlochen Golf Club.

🇹 The first loop is an easy, mostly flat, 2.5 miles with a mile of Lake Dubonet shoreline. You do cross two dirt roads, which can sometimes have traffic; be sure to check first. At signpost 2, head right and cross the earthen dam.

🇹 The second loop is 3.75 miles and follows the formation of the river, circles the Lost Lake basin, while passing a couple of large bogs. Once you cross the dam, follow the trail from post 3 to post 4. The trail follows along a small ridge above the valley, where the beginning of Platte River rushes away from the dam. From post 4, go through post 5 around to post 6, then back to post 3. You cross over the earthen dam once more, and proceed from post 2 back to the trailhead parking lot. This hike is around 6.7 miles.

🇹 If you want to hike just the second loop, park on the north side of the earthen dam. Begin and return to signpost 3.

12

Arcadia Dunes

the first UA trail

Looking for an easy hike up to a great dune overlook?

Guess what—one actually exists now.

The Grand Traverse Regional Land Conservancy (GTRLC) opened its first designated universally accessible (UA) trail on Arcadia Dunes in 2017. At the time, it was believed to be the first UA trail leading to a dunes overlook along the Michigan coast, according to executive director Glen Chown.

The overlook at the Arcadia Dunes from the first UA trail along northern Michigan's lakeshore.

For some time, it had been a goal to add a trail that would allow persons of all abilities—including those with mobility disabilities and slow-moving pedestrian traffic like the elderly, small youngsters, and families using infant strollers—to access a dune overlook.

"We have all of these wonderful, scenic dunes overlooks along the Lake Michigan coast, with our preserves like Old Baldy, Green Point Dunes, and Elberta Dunes South, and trails leading to them. However, although our conservancy trails vary widely, they all have natural features that make it impossible for a person with a mobility disability, or using a mobility device, to access the trails," Chown said at the time.

"We found accessibility at Arcadia Dunes, where we could build approximately a half-mile UA trail that leads to a beautiful deck and overlook on a bluff 300 feet above the lake. There's nothing else along the lakeshore that we know of that offers this kind of accessibility. We anticipate that it is going to be very popular as word gets out," the longtime director enthused.

Word has gotten out. I'm a frequent visitor to Arcadia Dunes, and the parking lot, which offers trails to access both the new UA overlook and the natural trails to Old Baldy Dune, frequently has cars in it. Some hikers are there to view both, but I've also seen families with little ones and many older people walking slowly up the UA trail to the Arcadia overlook.

The trail is composed of compacted crushed stone, boardwalks, and a series of switchbacks to maintain an easy manageable grade throughout its length. There are also benches along the way up the trail placed at scenic locations for a quick rest if needed.

The trail allows everyone to experience firsthand the flora, fauna, and views of Arcadia Dunes. It's six feet wide, and climbs through wooded dunes to the viewing platform.

The trail cuts through the trees closely enough for the visually impaired to feel their surfaces and experience the surroundings.

The platform overlook is large and offers several benches, including a couple of very comfortable rocking benches. The platform—300 feet above the lake—hangs out over a bluff with jaw-dropping views of the shoreline far below. Looking north, you can trace the shoreline around Betsie Bay, past the Frankfort harbor, and all the way to Point Betsie. You can also see Green Point Dunes and Elberta Dunes South rising high above the lakeshore.

It's a wonderful place to take a snack, sit back, and drink in that exceptional scenery—especially if you thought you might never be able to make the trek. Take advantage of this new opportunity, and don't forget your camera.

Terrell's Trail Notes

T The half-mile UA trail is marked, and takes off right from the parking area. It's a scenic, easy climb up to the platform deck overlooking the lake. The hard surface of the trail and boardwalks will accommodate people with mobility disability or using a mobility device. It also allows families with toddlers and babies to easily push a stroller up to the overlook.

13

Timbers Recreation Area

a scenic hiking and UA trail

The Timbers Recreation Area is one of my new favorite go-to spots for a quick, scenic hike. But, I have a feeling that it's yet to be discovered by a lot of area park users.

The 250-acre preserve is protected by the Grand Traverse Regional Land Conservancy, and is owned by Long Lake Township. It became a recreation area in 2014.

Old barn and silo at Timbers Recreation Area decked out with a glazed brick finish. Meat mogul J. Ogden Armour owned this property as a backwoods retreat in the early 1900s.

The unique property has around 9,000 feet of water frontage—2,000 feet on Long Lake, 20 acres on Fern Lake, plus frontage on Page Lake.

A universal access trail was added in 2020, which includes a crushed aggregate pathway, boardwalk, and fishing platform on Fern Lake.

The property has a long, interesting history. In the early 1900s, it was the backwoods retreat for meat mogul J. Ogden Armour and his family. In the 1960s, it became a Girl Scout camp. The camp operated until 2009, and then conservancy and township were able to team up and acquire the parcel with the assistance of Michigan Resources Trust Fund. Some of the old buildings from the Armour era still remain—a barn and silo decked out in handsome glazed brick is a stunning sight as you first head down trails from the parking lot.

A few reminders from the Girl Scouts also remain as you hike the trails. There are some boarded-up administrative and common buildings, as well as wooden platforms scattered through the forest that once supported their large canvas tents. They don't really detract from the area; they are just a reminder of what was here over the past century.

Old trails and two-tracks meander across the property, heading down to Long Lake, around Fern Lake, and into the upland meadows and forests. You stumble across the past as you hike around the preserve. The remnant of a beautiful old stone bridge suddenly appears along an old two-track near Long Lake. Dark, fern-filled hemlock woods surround the lakes. As you hike towards a picturesque forest canopy filled with maples and beeches, you'll find upland meadows covered with blackberry bushes and fields of waist-high grass.

It's not a long hike—around 2.5 miles— but the different zones range from wetlands, to lakes, hemlock forests, upland meadows and a hardwood forest.

The property has both ecological and historical value to Long Lake Township and area residents, especially many former Girl Scout attendees with memories of summer camps. Former staff members and campers helped raise funds to purchase the Timbers Recreation Area so it could be preserved. The land also offers important protection to the water quality of the Long Lake watershed.

Terrell's Trail Notes

T The trailhead is a short distance down Timber's Trail, off N. Long Lake Road. I like to hike counterclockwise from signpost A towards F. From there, I come to post 7, and continue towards post 6, which is at the dock to Long Lake, looking out at the lake's prominent islands. The trail changes from a two-track back to a trail as it meanders around the Long Lake shoreline for a while, passing a picnic area.

T Once the trail swings away from the lake, heading towards post 5, Fern Lake will come into view through the hemlock forest. From post 5 through post 2, you can either stay on the main trail, or take some side spurs that will add about a half a mile to your trek.

T Upon reaching post 2—and enjoying a stop at a picnic table with a delightful view of Fern Lake—I like to go uphill a short distance to post C. From there, it's an amiable walk across a wildflower-filled meadow to the cool canopy of the forest. On a hot summer day, this makes for a pleasant last mile back to the parking area.

14

Alligator Hill

after the storm

In early August 2015, hurricane-like winds hit the coast of Leelanau County, leveling much of the beautiful, old forest that covered Alligator Hill. It took about four months for the trails to the top to reopen, and I got my first look at the damage on Christmas Day, 2015.

The storm didn't affect the jaw-dropping view from the top.

I think shock was my first emotion. As I followed the cleared trail counterclockwise up to the top, there was virtually was no forest left. Just about every tree had either been blown over or snapped in two. The trail used to be covered by the canopy of beautiful, mature beech-maple forest and pine plantations. The landscape has been changed for the rest of my lifetime, and probably for my grandchildren's, too. Tears came to my eyes.

It was surreal, like I was hiking through a war-torn landscape that had been repeatedly shelled, or one that was leveled by a fierce hurricane. With winds that the National Weather Service estimated topped 100 miles per hour for a brief time, a hurricane may be the best analogy.

There were a good number of people on that Christmas Day also hiking the trails to see the damage. Three years after the windstorm, I went back up to see what it looked like. Once again, on a weekend after Labor Day, there were many other hikers. Many I spoke with weren't aware of the storm, but figured something unusual had happened, which as a storyteller, I recounted for them. My dog, Lulu, who was on leash with me, thought I was talking way too much and occasionally tugged at me to keep hiking.

Now, years after the storm, the undergrowth has hidden some of the twisted tree trunks, although the hike up the hill is mostly in sunlight now. It used to be a pleasant hike on hot, sunny days under the forest canopy. No more. And that probably won't bode well for cross country skiing either. Those trails are angled to receive direct afternoon winter sun—a death knell for lingering snow.

Once you reach the top, take the 1.6-mile over-and-back trail to Big Glen Lookout. The storm opened several scenic views of Lake Michigan and the Big Glen Lake shorelines that weren't there before.

The Manitou Islands Lookout—where on a calm, clear day you might also see Beaver and South Fox islands—hasn't changed

much. It still offers wonderful views of the forest stretching out below you to the Lake Michigan shoreline, distant dunes along Sleeping Bear Point, and the islands floating on the blue horizon. Both overlooks provide benches so you can sit and drink in those stunning views.

Starting up the trail from the trailhead you pass the remains of concrete kilns that lumberman Pierce Stocking built in the 1950s to make charcoal from the wood waste from his selective lumbering on Alligator Hill. Before that, in the 1920s, the property was a resort with an 18-hole golf course. You can still see faint outlines of some of the old fairways on the hillsides.

Alligator Hill makes a good hike, with the reward being two wonderful scenic overlooks. You won't be disappointed. Just don't pick a hot, steamy, sunny day where you might want relief from the sun.

Terrell's Trail Notes

- The trailhead is off Stocking Road—which is above M-109, between Glen Arbor and Glen Haven. It's a short hike from the trailhead up to where the circular trail takes off either right or left. It's 1.3 miles either way to the top. If you go right, you will pass a couple intersecting hiking trails that are rated intermediate and advanced.

- It's a little under 5 miles following the easy trail to the two lookouts and back down. When they say easy, they're comparing it to the intermediate and advanced trails—you still get a good workout on the long, steady climb to the top and back down.

This photo, taken in 1970, shows one of the old farms from Bay View. Sleeping Bear Dunes was created as a National Lakeshore that year, and this farm has been preserved as part of the park.

15

Bay View Trail

a view of Manitou Passage

As any summer visitor to Sleeping Bear Dunes National Lakeshore soon discovers, the most popular overlooks are normally packed with people.

The northern portion of the Bay View Trail—with its trailhead on Thorenson Road, just off M-22 —is not known for impressive dune panoramas. However, in my opinion, it offers one of the most scenic views in the park from Lookout Point. And in all the years I've been enjoying this beautiful vista, I've only encountered a handful of people.

The northern section covers the Farms Trail, Ridge Trail, Olsen Farm Trail, and a portion of the Heritage Trail system, offering a hike of around 2.5 miles. It does have some climbing, but how else would you expect to access those outstanding views? The climb isn't as hard as what you find at Empire Bluff or Pyramid Point. It's also one of only three trails in the Port Oneida Rural Historic District, and it passes the Olsen Farm, Miller Barn, and the old Port Oneida one-room schoolhouse.

The way I like to hike it is to head right for the overlook from the trailhead parking lot. It's a little over a half a mile of mostly steady, moderate climbing to Lookout Point, perched on a grassy knoll over 200 feet above Lake Michigan. There's a bench to sit and enjoy the almost a 360-degree panorama of the Manitou Islands, Pyramid Point, Sleeping Bear Point, beautiful lake vistas, historic farms, more tall hills to the south, and a shimmering glint of Glen Lake through a notch in the hills. The magnificent views are well worth the climb.

It's frequently windy on the knoll, which feels good on a hot summer day while you sit and drink in that bird's-eye view. I've often seen freighters heading up and down the lake through the treacherous Manitou Passage between the islands and mainland. Over 50 ships are believed to have gone down since the 1800s. It's one of the better places in the park to observe the big ships along the Sleeping Bear coastline with a pair of binoculars.

The northern section of the Bay View Trail offers a pleasant hike through forest and meadows, great views, and the historic charm of the farms and community that existed over a century ago. Fall offers all that plus some great autumn colors, especially when you look inland from Lookout Point. Just make sure you pick a sunny, windless day. Fall coolness coupled with a strong north wind that hasn't seen a windbreak since the UP can feel downright cold that time of year. That's why I like it best in summertime.

Terrell's Trail Notes

T Head north, across Thorenson Road, from the trailhead parking lot, and after a half a mile of fairly steady climbing—not steep—you come to signpost 1. Head right, up the hill, and you'll quickly reach Lookout Point with its panoramic views of lake and countryside.

T When you're ready to leave, either backtrack the short distance down the hill and continue around the Farms Trail, taking you by the Miller Barn and the Port Oneida Schoolhouse to post 3, or take the Ridge Trail at post 2 down to post 3. The Ridge Trail is marked one-way coming up, but that's for cross country ski season when you wouldn't want to go down a trail that has some steeper sections. Hiking isn't a problem. It's about a mile to the post via the Farms Trail, and a half a mile via the Ridge Trail. The trail descends on a knife-like ridge through a beautiful forest, quiet and scenic.

T From post 3, follow the Heritage Trail for about a mile past the historic Olsen Farm to post 4, crossing Thorenson Road. From there, it's about .1 miles to the parking lot.

In 1960, the S.S. Morazan ran aground off the shore of South Manitou Island.

16

Pyramid Point

**stunning views
and fewer crowds**

Summertime view areas along Sleeping Bear Dunes National Lakeshore can be crowded, and finding a peaceful spot to enjoy the vista isn't always easy.

Sometimes it seems like standing-room-only at popular spots along the Scenic Drive or at popular beaches in Empire and Glen Arbor. And the Dune Climb can look like a busy anthill.

One of my favorite spots among the perched dunes is the Pyramid Point overlook. Not that you won't find people and occasional crowds, but most of the time it's just a few other hardy souls. It's a long, continuous climb from the trailhead parking lot on Basch Road to the view area, and more climbing involved for other trails.

The reward is one of the most panoramic vistas you'll find along the National Lakeshore, which is well worth the strenuous ascent.

Once you reach the top, you step through the stunted trees into a real dune world. No boardwalks or roped off areas, just sand, often sculpted by the wind. A vista of white sand, blue water and sky greets you. The Manitou Islands float in the sea of blue. It's arguably one of the best island views in the National Lakeshore. I often find people just sitting in the sand, staring out at the lake and islands. After the hike up, it's a nice reward.

From the parking area, the trail climbs 225 feet to the overlook, which is a little over 300 feet above lake level. Hang gliders have launched off the steep dune from the top. I'll keep my feet on the ground, sitting in the sand, and just enjoy the panorama.

Many people will make the short hike from the trailhead to just enjoy the view, then head back down without exploring more of the Point. It's only .6 miles to the top, but a pretty moderate climb the whole way. Going back down is no problem.

There are another 2 miles of trails that explore the backside of the dune, and a large meadow below the dune that was cleared for homesteads in the early 1900s. The land was abandoned in the 1930s because the sandy soil wasn't good for farming. Unofficial trails also lead east from the top of the dune out along the ridge to more dunes without going down to the lake.

You will also see sandy trails leading down the backside of the dune to rejoin the mapped trails.

A sign at the top of the dune warns you to not go down the face of the dune to lake level. It's dangerous, ecologically detrimental, and with current high lake levels, there is no beach. If you have to be rescued after going down the face of the dune, you will be charged hefty fees.

Terrell's Trail Notes

🚩 The trailhead is located on Basch Road, which can be reached via Port Oneida Road, off M-22. The trailhead, complete with maps and privy, sits in a grassy meadow filled with summer wildflowers. An old two-track—also the trail—heads up the meadow towards the wooded hills. At the first posted junction, continue climbing the left fork of trail to reach the overlook.

🚩 As you head out onto the top of the dune, North Manitou Island sits on the blue horizon straight ahead of you. Nestled off the sunset side of the island is South Manitou. The overlook takes in the whole of the treacherous Manitou Passage where over 50 Great Lakes schooners lie on the bottom of the lake.

🚩 Unmarked trails head east through the trees, offering more stunning views of the lakeshore and surrounding countryside. At the backside, the migrating dune is spilling sand down into the woods. If you follow the marked trail system back to that first posted junction, you can head over to post 2, underneath the backside of the dune, and out into the meadow. It's a little under a mile around the meadow and back to post 3 where you begin the uphill climb back up to Basch Road. Follow the road about a half a mile back to the trailhead.

17

Good Harbor

beach walking is good for the soul and the legs

I love walking on our Great Lakes beaches, but prefer a Tom Hanks's *Cast Away* kind of experience—a lonelier environment without a lot of people cluttering the landscape.

One of my favorite beach hikes is along Good Harbor Beach beneath the Pyramid Point Dune.

On a nice summer day, you may encounter hordes of people parking along Bohemia Road—off M-22—and walking down to the easily accessible beach that stretches in either direction for as far as you can see. People sometimes seem to line the beach for the same distance.

A dirt road takes off in either direction at the end of the paved portion paralleling the lake. Driving the dirt road, you can't see the beach in either direction, but people park along it and hoof the short distance through the woods to the beach.

For my hike, you have to drive 2.5 miles west to get away from the maddening crowd. Keep right when you come to a split, and the dirt road ends in a circle. I've found few people drive that distance when they can get to the beach more quickly and easier off the other paved access at Good Harbor Road.

Park around the circle, and a short trail leads back to the lake and—surprise—a bluff that rises about 25 feet or so above the beach and Lake Michigan. It's another reason you won't find lots of beach walkers at this point. At the end of the paved road, and for much of the dirt road heading west, there isn't any bluff, and that easier access is the attraction for many beachgoers who frequent that section.

When you reach the bluff and make the short descent down to the beach, you often won't see anybody. Occasionally, there will be a few people on the beach, never many. The beach lends itself to walking, rather than swimming, as it's somewhat rocky along the edge of the water.

As you stroll along the water's edge, colors sparkle from rocks and pebbles scattered along the beach. Piles of driftwood lay gleaming white like ancient whale bones washed on shore, bleached and ground smooth by eons of water, weather, and sand. The Manitou Islands are nestled just off the coast. Sunlight glints off small waves lapping on the soft sand. The sun warms your skin and gentle breezes ruffle your hair.

Gulls fly above with cries filling the air. Some dive into the water hoping to snatch a snack.

The mesmerizing pleasures of sight, sound, and feel are always a delight. It's so relaxing that I often get lost in thought. But, what better place could you find to sit on a clump of dune grass, or a piece of driftwood, and watch the day slowly creep by. That's what I call a "happy place."

Bonfires are allowed on this beach, so pack some dry wood and pick up a bottle of wine from Good Harbor Vineyards for a romantic evening with the Pure Michigan sunset.

Terrell's Trail Notes

T You can walk as far as the Lake Michigan high water levels allow you, which used to be under Pyramid Point Dune. As of the summer of 2020, you were stopped well short of being able to do that. It's still a pleasant, scenic beach walk, and walking in sand always stretches your leg muscles a little bit more.

18

Clay Cliffs

scenic views of two lakes

One of the newer natural areas in the Leelanau Conservancy stable, Clay Cliffs Natural Area, has quickly become one of my favorite areas for a quick, scenic hike any time of year.

I've hiked and snowshoed up to the overlook with breath-catching views of Lake Michigan, the Leelanau shoreline, and the Manitou Islands floating at the edge of sky and lake. It's not a long trek, just a little over 1.5 miles round trip, but a good climb to the bluff and the overlook that sits more than 200 feet above the lake. After lingering at the well-constructed overlook—complete with bench seating—to drink in that view, more stunning scenery lies ahead.

The trail continues along the wooded bluff before exiting the forest to cross a large, grassy meadow. As you cross, views of azure Lake Leelanau stretch across the bottom half of the horizon. About halfway across the meadow, a well-placed bench offers a scenic respite to enjoy the sparkling lake views. The trail continues to drop through the meadow before coming to a bluff above the lower woods. You'll drop down into this before heading back to the parking lot.

The clay cliffs are a unique feature and rare along the Michigan lakeshore. Eagles nest here, and can sometimes be seen from the overlook. The 105-acre property is owned by Leland Township and managed by the conservancy.

Spring is a special time in the natural area. "It's one of the most prolific wildflower sites in the county, and the trillium-filled woods are beautiful in early spring when Dutchman's breeches and spring beauties start coming up," preserve manager Becky Hill told me. "The conservancy conducts guided hikes on the property throughout the year, and spring is always a popular hike."

Terrell's Trail Notes

T The trailhead is located off M-22, a few miles north of Leland. The trail is well marked and easy to follow. In a short distance, you come to the first of five intersections. Head right at each intersection to follow the loop. You climb the bluff through the woods and return across the meadow so you can enjoy the panoramic view of beautiful Lake Leelanau.

T The first portion of the trail is flat as you approach tall hills ahead. Take a sharp right at the second intersection and proceed to climb through the woods to the top of the bluff. Once you reach the top of the forested bluff, it's a quick trek over to the short out-and-back overlook spur. The panoramic view takes center stage.

T Heading back, follow the trail, again right. Shortly, it exits the woods and starts a long trek across the open meadow, affording scenic Lake Leelanau views. There are a couple of large stakes along the trail for winter use in case of deep snow. This was an old homestead with farm fields long ago. When you reach the line of woods across the bottom of the meadow, it's the top of a bluff. Descend through the forest to an intersection, proceed right, and in a little under a half a mile you'll reach the parking lot.

T The trail system is nicely spaced. You don't see people heading down as you go up, and vice-versa. Road noise, although nearby, is left behind once you enter the woods and start climbing the bluff. In late afternoon, the slanting sun highlights the trees, the bluff, the shoreline, and Lake Leelanau on the way down.

19

Houdek Dunes

a mini version
of Sleeping Bear Dunes

One of my favorite Leelanau Conservancy Natural Areas is Houdek Dunes, which offers a wonderful hike through ancient forests, along shifting sand dunes, and beautiful creeks. You also learn a little bit about the peninsula's geological formation by following self-guided hiking maps.

Houdek Dunes Natural Area, located off M-22 just a few miles north of Leland, is a microcosm of nearby Sleeping Bear Dunes National Lakeshore and its dune environment.

Visitors pause beneath
the ancient sugar maple.

A quarter of a mile inland from Lake Michigan, there are active and stabilized dunes; open, pitted, and perched sand dunes; and even a few blowout dunes. It's exactly what you find at Sleeping Bear, just not as big and towering. What you won't find are the huge throngs of people visiting the national park during the summer.

As you hike through the 370-acre preserve, what is really striking to me are the large trees scattered along the trails and throughout the natural area. Stands of huge, bright, healthy white birches, many over a century old, can be found throughout Houdek Dunes. These ancient giants are highly unusual for this transition species.

"You don't find many birches elsewhere that are this old," said Jenee Rowe, a land steward with the conservancy. "Woodland pockets created by dips in the dunes shelter the birches from the harsh wind and allow them to thrive. There are also large red oaks, cottonwood, red pine, and sugar maples scattered among the dunes in sheltered valleys. Many of them also appear to be at least a century old, and some older than that."

An ancient sugar maple with a huge canopy is located about 1.8 miles from the trailhead, following the Forest Trail. (If you want a short hike, take the Crossover Trail—it's only about a three-quarters of a mile.) Sit beneath its massive limbs on a bench, relax, and enjoy the peaceful rustling sound of leaves in the breeze. It is a wonderful spot to get in tune with nature.

"We don't know for sure how old the tree is, but I've heard estimates of 150 to 200 years old," exclaimed Rowe when we paused for a rest. "It was probably at least a seedling when the first European settlers arrived to homestead this region."

The last time I was there, in 2016, the tree had started failing and losing branches. It was sad to see.

Terrell's Trail Notes

▼ I recommend hiking the entire outside trail around the natural area, which includes the rugged Ridgeline Trail that splits off the Forest Trail a little over a mile into the hike. It's up and down with roots to watch out for, but a nice hike through mature, forested backdunes. You pass over the highest point in the preserve, and it eventually leads to an overlook of swift-flowing Houdek Creek—a beautiful spring-fed trout stream that is the primary tributary flowing into North Lake Leelanau.

▼ From there it's less than half a mile to the ancient sugar maple and bench, then another half a mile back to the parking lot. In total, you hike around three miles, round trip. You often have the back portions of the linked trails all to yourself, especially the Ridgeline, if other hikers are in the area.

▼ The trails are well marked with detailed maps located at every intersection, including the length of the trail ahead. As one of the conservancy's largest preserves, the trails spread out nicely. The preserve is also popular in the winter for snowshoeing.

▼ Once you climb the short set of stairs at the trailhead and enter the dunes environment, it's a different, peaceful world. Traffic noise and the hustle and bustle of M-22 are left behind.

Fred Tank,
the longtime caretaker
of Power Island.

20

Power Island

boating, hiking, camping, and geocaching

Grand Traverse county park Power Island is popular with boaters and kayakers. It sits a little over 2.5 miles off Old Mission Peninsula's Bower Harbor in West Grand Traverse Bay.

It's also one of the top geocaching spots on the planet. Considered a Holy Grail of caches, it draws geocachers from all around the world. When the sport began in 2000, Power Island was one of the original 75 geocaching locations. Today, there are over 2.7 million locations hidden around the world, and the number grows daily. But this island remains a top draw.

On warm summer days, it also becomes the go-to gathering place for Traverse City's motorboat set. They tend to raft together off the eastern and southeast shores, out of the typical prevailing, westerly breezes. The 200-acre park that rises over 150 feet above the bay is also a magnet for kayakers on light wind days. There are ten primitive campsites, a boat dock, picnic areas, and about 6 miles of trails that lead up to the top of the island and over to the rocky western side.

I'm not a motor boater, but every few years I get a yearn to visit the island to hike its trails. I watch for light wind days, when I know it will be safe to kayak across the open water. My last outing in 2019 occurred the weekend after Labor Day: hot, sunny, and windless.

I waited until early afternoon to make the crossing and it was a pleasant paddle across the glass-like bay. All the motorboats had already arrived and rafted. Once at the island, I paddled by Basset Island; there were kayakers camping there, enjoying the end of the beautiful, summer weather.

Heading to the beach, I pulled my kayak ashore to begin hiking. I had to weave through the maze of anchored boats and swimming dogs. While the aquatic party prevails with people laughing, splashing, and music floating across the water, solitary souls can find tranquility, even on the busiest days. Most of the motorboat set never venture more than a few yards from the water's edge.

The interior of the island is a treat for hikers. Well-maintained trails lead through a dense forest to Basset Island, or climb the high ridgeline that can easily be seen from the mainland. You can hike up to Eagle's Nest, a great lookout along the rocky western bluff that offers panoramic views of the bay and Leelanau shoreline.

Much of the thanks for the well-maintained trails go to longtime island caretaker/park ranger Fred Tank, a retired NMC professor, who has been spending summers on the island

with his wife, Tina, since 1986. They come over in May and stay until October in a cabin that has solar-powered electricity. I always look forward to a chat with them before taking off on my hike.

How many counties offer an island park for their citizens to hang out on, explore, and even camp on if so inclined? Not many. Enjoy the opportunity.

Terrell's Trail Notes

- There's a map at the trailhead, which is just beyond the dock and beach area. Once you leave that area, you'll pass the ranger's cabin and begin to climb up the flank of the ridge. You'll come to a split—you head over to Basset Island or continue climbing the ridge. There really aren't any distances posted, but it's around a mile up to Eagle's Nest and its panoramic vista of West Bay and Leelanau Peninsula.

- The trail continues across the top of the island, where you'll encounter many large trees that survived lumbering because of their remote location. It's a beautiful canopy to walk under. Trails lead off across the top, or you can head down the western side of the bluff to the lake and beach level. That's where a geocache is allegedly located, but I didn't find it.

- Trails continue to circle for a couple of miles around the southern tip of the island, offering stunning views down the bay towards Traverse City, before leading back to the dock area. In all, my fitness tracker said I had hiked over 5 miles.

- The bay was still tranquil as I started my paddle back to Bowers Harbor. It had been a good day on land and water.

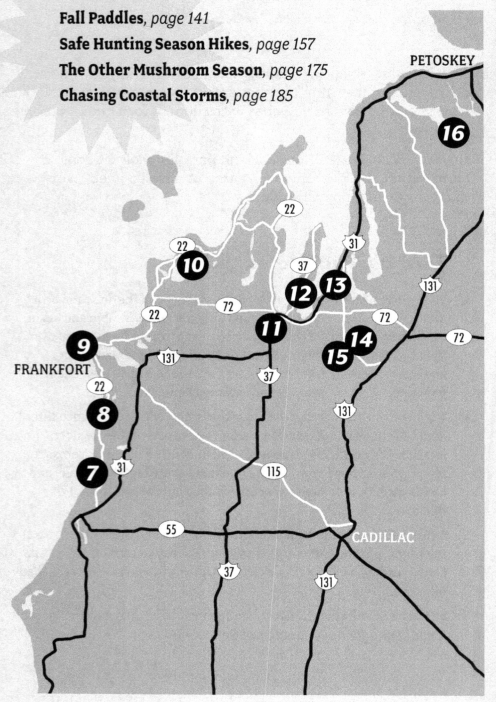

See also
Fall Paddles, *page 141*
Safe Hunting Season Hikes, *page 157*
The Other Mushroom Season, *page 175*
Chasing Coastal Storms, *page 185*

PETOSKEY

FRANKFORT

CADILLAC

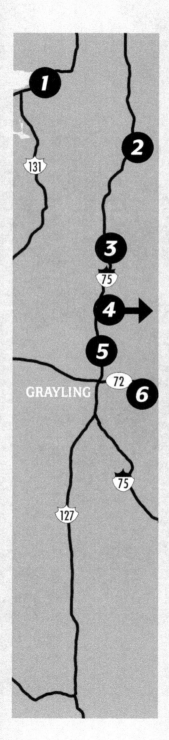

Autumn

A fall paddle leads to some of the best colors

In northern Michigan, fall colors and rivers go together like ice cream and cones. One is good, but both create an exquisite combination.

Take a sunny day, a river, and add a tint of fall color. The river often reflects and enhances the effect, creating beautiful double images. A fall paddle is a relaxing way to kick back and enjoy the kaleidoscope as you float downstream. It's a different kind of fall tour.

Here are some of my favorite floats on three of our popular rivers: the Au Sable, South Branch of the Au Sable, and Manistee. These rivers yield a variety of brilliant colors, great scenery, and can be enjoyed by both beginning and experienced paddlers. I've included a listing of liveries that service the rivers.

Paddlers on the Au Sable River during fall.

THE AU SABLE is known for its gentle current, clean water, and north woods setting. It starts narrow in Grayling, but quickly widens as the East Branch joins the main river before crossing under I-75. Cottages become less frequent and the shoreline alternates between high and low banks with lots of hardwoods for color. Popular trips from Grayling are to Burton's Landing—8 miles and around a three-hour paddle; and Stephan Bridge Landing—a 13-mile, four-hour trip.

THE SOUTH BRANCH OF THE AU SABLE River offers a popular 10-mile float from Chase Bridge down to Smith Bridge (M-72). It takes about five hours, depending on how many stops you make. This section of river passes through the Mason Tract, a nearly 5,000-acre preserve kept in a natural state. The undeveloped preserve is forested in pines and hardwoods that provide a colorful backdrop for a fall trip. The South Branch splits the middle of the tract, providing one of the most scenic, peaceful floats in northern Michigan.

Two popular stops along the trip are the remains of Durant's Castle and the Mason Chapel. Both are marked with signs on the river. The 42-room castle burned down completely in the early 1930s and was never rebuilt. The Mason Chapel, a beautiful, quiet spot of reverence, was built in 1960.

THE MANISTEE RIVER, one of the longest rivers in the state at 163 miles, offers many paddling opportunities. Two of the best locations for fall color are between U.S. 131 and the Harvey Road Bridge takeout near Mesick. Both sections snake through a long, wide valley, often rimmed by high, sandy bluffs and an ever-present hardwood forest that offers breathtaking shades of color. The river is wide, with an easy-flowing current that allows for plenty of leaf peeping. The reflections of fall color in the deeper, slower pools along the river can be brilliant—a double-down view.

One Manistee float trip begins at the rest area at the U.S. 131 Bridge and continues to Baxter Bridge access—a 10.5-mile float that takes about four hours. The second trip goes from Baxter Bridge down to Harvey Bridge and features beautiful, unspoiled scenery, often under high banks. It's an arduous, 20-mile, six-hour paddle, but ever-changing collage of fall colors makes it worthwhile.

Liveries

All rent canoes and kayaks, and most will offer a spotting service if you have your own equipment.

AU SABLE RIVER LIVERIES LOCATED IN GRAYLING

- Borchers Outfitters, www.canoeborchers.com or 989-348-4921
- Penrod's Canoe and Kayak, www.penrodscanoe.com or 888-467-4837
- Carlisle Canoe Livery, www.carlislecanoelivery.com or 989-344-1400
- Long's Canoe Livery, 989-348-7224
- Ray's Canoe Livery, 989-348-5844

SOUTH BRANCH OF THE AU SABLE LIVERIES LOCATED JUST NORTH OF ROSCOMMON

- Campbell's Canoe Livery, www.canoeatcampbells.com or 800-722-6633
- Paddle Brave Canoe Livery, www.paddlebrave.com or 989-275-5273

MANISTEE RIVER

- Chippewa Landing, www.chippewalanding.com or 231-313-0832, located at Chippewa Landing Trail
- Wilderness Canoe Trips, www.manisteerivertrips.com or 231-885-1485, located in Mesick

1

Skyline Trail

a cabin in the sky

This is one of my favorite locations in northern Michigan for a grand panoramic view, especially in fall. The view stretches from the observation deck along the Skyline Trail to Lake Michigan, Petoskey, Harbor Springs, and Little Traverse Bay. It reminds me of catching a bird's-eye view from an overlook along the Blue Ridge trail.

The view from the porch of a cabin on the Skyline Trail. What a sunset view this would be

It's not hard to imagine that you might be hiking along a forest trail in the Blue Ridge Mountains as you traverse the switchback North Country Trail (NCT), heading over to the short Skyline Trail spur. This relatively new section of the NCT, opened in 2010, crosses a tall moraine that rises over 600 feet above Lake Michigan and the city of Petoskey. Hiking along switchbacks, you look down into a forest that drops endlessly away. Not being able to see any bottomlands, it's easy to pretend that you're hiking along a mountainside.

The NCT is a long-distance hiking trail that runs 4,600 miles from the Vermont/New York border to the middle of North Dakota. Around 1,100 miles trek across the Wolverine State's two peninsulas.

The observation deck offers panoramic views that stretch to the lake and across Little Traverse Bay to the tall hills that house the Boyne Highlands and Nub's Nob ski areas. You can look across the Bear River Valley and at the farms nestled between the lower hills above Lake Michigan. This is the first time long-distance hikers heading west on the North Country Trail will see Lake Michigan.

It's a little under a mile from the parking area on top of the moraine to the overlook spur. A short, well-marked spur trail leads over to the platform in the sky.

A new wrinkle was added in 2018 when a small cabin was erected to serve as a walk-in shelter for use along the NCT. It's free, with a two-night maximum stay rule. The cabin was constructed by a collection of local volunteers and the property owner. The spur trail up to the cabin leaves the NCT at about the same point as the spur for the observation deck. It's a short climb up to the cabin, which is located in a clearing with a firepit beside it. You have to call a phone number listed on the door to get the combination to open the lock so they know it's being used. The view from the deck is worth the short hike. It looks out over a wide swath of the Bear River valley to large hills on the other side. You can day hike from the cabin.

Terrell's Trail Notes

▼ The towering moraine is visible from U.S. 131 as you head north from Walloon Lake. Take Bear River Road a short distance east from 131 over to River Road, then north to Click Road. Head east to Cedar Valley Road, which ends at Greenwood Road. Turn right and follow it around a curve to a four-way intersection. Continue straight through, and it becomes Brubaker Road, which you follow to Krause Road. Take that, and in less than 2 miles, the parking area for the Skyline Trail is on the right. It's not as confusing as it sounds.

▼ A trail heads west from the parking area and quickly joins the NCT. Head right and in less than a mile you reach the spur trails for both the observation deck and the cabin. The NCT is well marked and easy to follow. The trail is a bit rugged with a good uphill return.

The cabin along the Skyline portion of the North Country Trail.

2

Green Timbers

fall color and bugling elk

Fall is the time to visit the Green Timbers Quiet Area—a beautiful 6,400-acre tract of grasslands, pockets of pine and hardwood, and the wild Sturgeon River running through it. It's part of the Pigeon River Country State Forest.

A woman and her dog camping in Green Timbers fills a water bag from the Sturgeon River.

Two good reasons for a visit in late September and early October are the chances to see elk and the emerging fall colors, both of which can be dazzling. Sometimes, I've gotten a glimpse of elk, but not always. The symphony of brilliant red, orange, and yellow trees that dot the grasslands and edge the forest never fail to steal your breath.

Green Timbers is a combination of second-growth timber and open grassland, crisscrossed with old two-tracks that now serve as trails for hiking, mountain biking, and horseback riding. The terrain is mostly rolling on the west side, sloping down to the Sturgeon River valley. A high ridge overlooks the east side.

"September and early October is when we start getting reports that elk and deer are being spotted in Green Timbers. They are coming into the area to feed," DNR employee Joe Valentine, with the Atlanta Field Office at the time, told me years ago. "It's also the time of year when elk start to rut and bugle. The best time to see them is a little before sunset, and they are more active on cooler days. If it's warm, they tend to stay put during daylight hours, but they'll come out to feed."

There are two entrances into the tract. I like the one off Fontinalis Road, which is about 7 miles east of Vanderbilt and the first named road heading north you come to once you leave the village. The other entrance, off Sturgeon Valley Road, leads to a viewing area along a ridge on the east side of the river. The trails don't connect; that's another chapter.

Terrell's Trail Notes

🮵 As you drive back on Fontinalis Road, look for a locked gate on the right side of the road guarding a two-track leading back into a large meadow. The parking area is designated by a circular ring of boulders.

🮵 It's about a 2.75-mile trek down to the river from the parking area. The 5.5-mile round trip is an easy, beautiful hike with lots of leaf-peeping opportunity. Pockets of trees scattered across the descending grasslands offer eye-catching bursts of color.

🮵 Follow the two-track across the meadow and around a corner with a few trees, and enter another large grassland area that is sometimes planted with rotating food crops—a big attraction for elk and deer. If you go looking to see elk, the grassy hillsides overlooking the plot make a great place to sit. Be patient, and you will possibly be rewarded with a close-up view of these magnificent animals. Don't forget to bring binoculars.

🮵 The two-track continues gently down the valley flanked by tall hills. Make sure you continue left on the two-track as you approach the river. A faint, old two-track appears to the right, but goes nowhere. A commercial-grade bridge crosses the river—probably left over from the McLouth Steel days when they owned the property before donating it to the state. It's a great place to relax and enjoy the sights and sounds of the river and the colorful forested hills bordering the river valley.

🮵 The trail used to continue across the bridge through a lowland area and up the ridge on the other side of the river. I don't think it leads anywhere today. It disappears into wetlands.

🮵 The trip back up to your vehicle is a gentle climb. If it's late afternoon, with the sun lower in the sky, the fall colors will be even more brilliant. Golden ferns alongside the path, glowing in the sun, light your way. This is not a well-known trail, but it's one of my favorite fall outings—with or without elk.

3

Aspen Park

**nice hiking
during hunting season**

Looking for a new place to hike and mountain bike safely during firearms deer hunting season?

Aspen Park in Gaylord has been around for some time, but about 20 years ago they added 2.5 miles of paved trails and over 6 miles of mountain bike trails—also open to hiking—that snake around the 100-acre park. Some trails are right along Gaylord's large, unique elk pen, where you can sometimes see the animals nonchalantly grazing or meandering around the enclosure. It's quite a sight to glimpse these noble animals strolling around the pen, but not always a guarantee in this 105-acre area.

If you fail to see any elk on the hike, go over to the nearby corner of Grandview and Elkview roads where the city feeds the animals. I've seen them at both locations. Seeing the males in the park with those magnificent racks always takes my breath away.

Aspen Park is located off the I-75 business loop at the end of Commerce Boulevard on the south side of town. It dead-ends at the trailhead parking area.

The paved trail takes off through a gate meant to keep vehicles out—not people—and heads into a wooded area of large maple, pine, and hemlock trees that are prevalent throughout the park. You quickly come to an intersection that offers three nice, easy hiking loops that total around 2 miles. One of these goes by the elk pen. An additional half mile of paved trail leads off the Hemlock Trail along its southern end, and drops down along scenic Scott's Pond. It has a bench where you can sit and enjoy the scenic serenity of this beautiful spot, tucked down and away from the often more crowded main trails up above.

The mountain bike trail constantly intersects the paved trail, and you can hike through the woods on portions of the trail, seeing even more of the park. I've encountered few mountain bikers on the trails in recent years.

The beauty of the area, the unusual terrain so close to town, and a chance to observe elk up close—what more could you ask for during deer hunting season?

Terrell's Trail Notes

- You can hike or mountain bike on all the trails, and they groom the 2-mile paved trail for cross country skiing during the winter.

- The paved trail takes off just beyond the kiosk in the parking area, at the end of Commerce Boulevard. It's a pretty easy trail for all three outdoor activities, and winds around on the level uplands terrain. The half-mile pond trail does have a climb from the pond back up to either Hemlock Trail or the end of Commerce Boulevard.

- The mountain bike trail off paved Elk Trail offers a couple of miles of nice hiking through pine stands and across open meadows. Once the trail makes a turn back to the west, you start encountering uneven terrain and some surprising hill climbs and switchbacks as you pass a couple of ponds on the west side of the paved trails. It's a surprisingly rugged portion of the park that you don't see from the paved trails.

Safe places to hike during deer hunting season

Rifle hunting deer season in the woods are one place nonhunters shouldn't be. Your safety is the main reason, and a rifle bullet can travel a good distance in the case of a miss. But, respect for the hunters who only have a narrow window of time to enjoy their sport is another good reason to avoid the woods. Nonhunters have the rest of the year to pursue their outdoor interests.

There are, however, several nice parklands managed by the Grand Traverse Conservation District that offer nice hiking opportunities near Traverse City. You won't even feel like you're near a city. Hunting isn't permitted at any of these sites.

The 140-acre Grand Traverse Commons Natural Area in the tall hills on the west side offers nice hiking trails with grand views as an added bonus. Four to five miles of trails—some covered with woodchips—wander up, down, around wooded hillsides, across streams, skirting meadows and wetlands. Trails are well marked with signposts at intersections with maps and colored arrows posted along the trails. A couple of overlooks have benches: one on Old Orchard Trail overlooks downtown and West Bay; another, on a spur off Copper Ridge Trail, overlooks the barns and distant hills. There are six trailheads scattered around the perimeter.

There's a plethora of hiking trails in Hickory Hills and Hickory Meadows. Stroll through the large meadow or hike up into the wooded hills for some wonderful panoramic views of West Bay and the city far below. It's a good climb and worth it for scene-stealing views.

On the south side of the city, the Grand Traverse Natural Education Reserve offers a few miles of interesting trails that overlook the Boardman River, now flowing free with the Sabin Dam removal. Trailheads are located at Oleson Bridge, Lone Pine off Keystone Road, and at the Nature Center off Cass Road. You can often spot wildlife, and especially waterfowl, along these short hikes.

Pelizzari Natural Area, on the east side of the city, is located at the base of Old Mission Peninsula. There are around 3 miles of trails that flow around an old orchard and the remnants of farm fields, through upland hardwood forests, and a section of old-growth hemlock forest above East Bay. Scenic and peaceful best describe this hike.

Brown Bridge Quiet Area, located about 12 miles southeast of Traverse City, offers several miles of trails from easy to strenuous. Deer hunting is not allowed in the core area that includes the two trails beginning from Ranch Rudolf Road and Brown Bridge Road. The easterly end of the property contains the 70-acre Grasshopper Creek Permit Hunting Area, a limited-permit-only hunting area regulated by the City of Traverse City. On the map, it is marked Trail 2 area. Best not to hike there during rifle hunting season.

The trails meander along a ridge with a couple of overlooks of the Boardman River snaking through the valley. You can also hike down along the river and through some of the wetland areas bordering the river. It's a strenuous climb back up out of the valley, but well worth it. The soothing sound of the river rushing down the valley creates a tranquil mood. You can occasionally spot eagles soaring over the valley.

Another interesting, safe hike is Michigan Legacy Art Park, located on a 30-acre preserve within the wooded hills of Crystal Mountain. There are 49 captivating sculptures representing aspects of life in the Wolverine State. About 3 miles of trails wind up and down the hills among the sculptures, making it a real hike, not just a stroll in the woods. The preserve is safely tucked away in the middle of the resort, which does not allow hunting.

The barns from one of the trails in the Grand Traverse Natural Area.

Rattlesnake Hills

great views, great name

I've always been willing to climb a northern Michigan hill for a good view, and I discovered many years ago that Rattlesnake Hills offers one of the most panoramic fall views in the northern Lower Peninsula. However, it was the name that first intrigued me.

I mean, who wouldn't be curious about a place dubbed Rattlesnake Hills?

Hikers enjoying the panoramic view from the top of the Rattlesnake Hills.

When I first saw the name after moving up here 40-some years ago, I quickly added it to the various places that I wanted to hike. It wasn't necessarily to find a massasauga rattlesnake—which I did think would be a plus—but I'd read about the panoramic vista from the top. Rattlesnake Hills are a portion of the High Country Pathway (HPC), circling about 77 miles around the Pigeon River Country State Forest. They lie along its southern edge, just northwest of Atlanta.

Before my first trip to hike the trail, I called the Gaylord DNR Field Office and spoke with their wildlife biologist. He told me that the snake was probably still in the area, but seldom seen.

"At one time early settlers must have seen a pretty good population of them in that area. They typically hibernate in swamps and wetland systems adjoining upland areas," he told me. "The area has been called that as far back as I can remember. There are still populations scattered around Lower Michigan, but the species has dwindled. Consider yourself lucky if you spot one."

Adult massasauga rattlesnakes are thick-bodied and can be 18- to 30-inches long. They are brown to grayish in color with large brown blotches on their back and smaller, lighter brown patches on their sides. Not considered aggressive, they avoid humans, but it's still best to give them wide berth and quickly seek attention if bitten. Like all rattlesnakes, their venom is poisonous.

I didn't find a massasauga on that first trip, or subsequent trips, but did find what I consider one of the most breathtaking fall overlooks in the Lower Peninsula. The hike to the top of the Hills isn't easy, but it's not a long hike. About a 3-mile hike out and back, and you pass another couple of nice views along the way. There are two hills before reaching the top of the third hill and that treasured vista.

From the top of the third hill—a bald knob—the bird's-eye view stretches as far as the eye can see. It's a 180-degree panoramic

scene that unfolds from the southwest to the northeast. Long, deep valleys and ridgelines blend into an endless horizon of colorful forest. It's one of the most beautiful landscapes that I've encountered among my many, many hikes around the Lower Peninsula.

I will sit for a long time just enjoying that view, especially after the effort it takes to get up there. The only thing that could have made it better would have been hearing bugling elk in the valleys below, which I haven't. Fall would be the time to possibly hear them.

Terrell's Trail Notes

🝨 It's about a two-hour drive from Traverse City to Atlanta. About 4 miles north of the village on M-33, you take off to the west on Rouse Road. It's about another 4 miles to where the HCP crosses the road and heads up the flank of the Rattlesnake Hills. You pass Elk Ridge Golf Course on the way. Blue-tipped, wooden slats mark the crossing, and blue paint splotches as well as blue triangles on trees mark the trail.

🝨 It's fairly easy to follow, but sometimes you have to look around for the trail markings to make sure you're heading in the right direction. A few two-tracks also cut through the area. The hike up the first hill is fairly easy. It's the hike up the second hill that's the most grueling of the climbs. The third hill tops out at a little over 1,200 feet above sea level, about 300 feet above the surrounding area.

🝨 The hike back down is a little easier and quicker, even though it still involves some climbing over those other two hills.

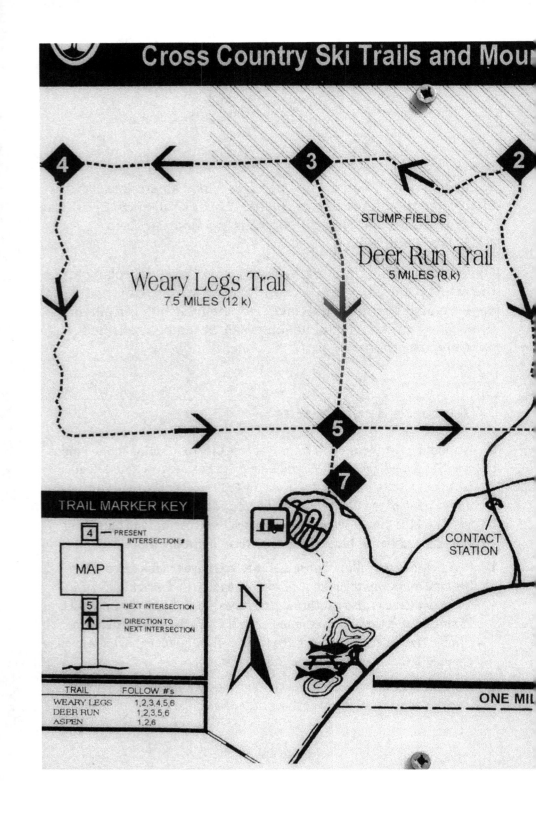

4

3

2

STUMP FIELDS

Deer Run Trail
5 MILES (8 k)

Weary Legs Trail
7.5 MILES (12 k)

5

7

CONTACT
STATION

TRAIL MARKER KEY

4 — PRESENT INTERSECTION #

MAP

5 — NEXT INTERSECTION

⬆ — DIRECTION TO NEXT INTERSECTION

TRAIL	FOLLOW #'s
WEARY LEGS	1,2,3,4,5,6
DEER RUN	1,2,3,5,6
ASPEN	1,2,6

N

ONE MIL

ike Trails DNR

en Trail
LES (4.9 k)

LOGGING
CAMP

- - - - - BIKE / SKI TRAIL
———— GRAVEL ROAD
======= PAVED ROAD
===== POOR DIRT ROAD
- - - - - FOOT TRAILS

8 INTERSECTION #

ACCESS SITE and
ACCESSIBLE FISHING

CAMPGROUND

PICNIC SHELTER

5

Hartwick Pines

bike or hike the Weary Legs Trail a colorful fall

One of my favorite fall trails at Hartwick Pines is the Weary Legs Trail which meanders 8 miles around the eastern portion of the Lower Peninsula's largest state park.

Most visitors to the park never see much of the trail. They come to visit the Forest Visitor Center and see the 49-acre forest of old-growth pines, which also contains the logging museum.

A paved trail winds through the section of old-growth white pine that somehow survived the lumbering era at the turn of the last century. Some of the pines are more than 300 years old and stand 130 feet tall. It's definitely impressive and merits visiting, but so does the rest of the state park.

Take a hike on portions of the Weary Legs Trail and you'll see many of the different habitats that make up the nearly 10,000-acre park. The 8-mile trail is divided into three sections with crossover trails offering lengths of 3, 5, and 8 miles. The terrain covers mostly small ridges and hills, although the last section, that winds out along I-75, has some longer climbs and descents.

This area, like most of northern Michigan, was logged around 1900, but the pines that have grown back and the mature hardwood forest are impressive and colorful this time of year. As you go around the trail you can also see history unfold if you look carefully. The 5-mile loop has many of the ancient white pine stumps scattered around the landscape, especially the crossover trail that forms the loop off the main trail. It's a reminder of the great forest that once stood here. One of the signposts—number 3—marks the site of a logging camp once located in the long valley between ridges. The crossover trail follows an old railroad spur that ran the length of the valley when lumbering was taking place.

Much of that valley is planted in tall grass that deer feed on. The golden grass waving in the wind is almost hypnotizing; it's like a sea with waves rippling across its golden surface. In fall, I sometimes just sit under a lone tree for a while watching it wave.

Fall is a great time to visit. The busy season is over and hiking the colorful, uncrowded trails is pure bliss.

Terrell's Trail Notes

▼ If you want to do the 8-mile trail you have to skip the mile crossover trail at signpost 3 and head on to 4. Continuing on around the extended loop, you begin a long climb into a hardwood forest that forms a "tunnel of trees." When you reach the top, it levels off. At signpost 4, the trail turns south and parallels the interstate for a mile. You don't see the interstate, but you can hear the traffic. Once you turn east, the trail rolls over small hills back to the trailhead as you pass intersecting crossover trails at signposts 5 and 6.

▼ The trailhead for the Weary Legs Trail is in the day-use area parking lot at the end of the park access road.

▼ You can either hike or mountain bike the trail, which is groomed for cross country skiing in the winter. The signposts are coordinated in colors for the three loops. I recommend the 3-mile Aspen Loop, marked with red, and Deer Run Loop—yellow signposts—for hiking.
The crossover trails are signposts 2 and 3. You continue straight ahead at the post to continue on the long loop.

6

Mason Tract Pathway

scenic, mystical, and historical

"Sportsman slow your pace... ahead lies the fabled land of the South Branch of the Au Sable River. Hunters, fishers, hikers, and skiers have roamed these hills in the solitude so beautifully offered. The land, rich in tradition, stands ready to revive your soul."

A close-up view of the South Branch of the Au Sable River from the Mason Tract Pathway.

These are a couple of lines from a plaque posted by the DNR at the beginning of the Mason Tract Pathway. The pathway honors George Mason, an industrialist, who bequeathed 1,500 acres to the state in the 1950s for hunting, fishing, recreation—with no development allowed. The original gift has been enlarged to nearly 5,000 acres protecting much of the revered Blue Ribbon trout stream, which is also popular with canoeists and kayakers.

This has been a favorite northern Michigan pathway from the time I first hiked it around 1980. Over the years, I've hiked and cross country skied the pathway numerous times.

The trailhead is just off M-72, about 15 miles east of Grayling. The pathway meanders along the west bank of the famed river for a little over 10 miles to Chase Bridge Road, which is a long hike on the out-and-back trail. The hike over to Durant's Castle covers about half the pathway, and in my opinion is the most scenic portion. Autumn is my favorite time of year to hike this area as it's less crowded, and the fall colors along the river really stand out.

Rather than hike back over the same route on the return, I take my mountain bike to Durant Castle and hide it near the landmark. I end up hiking a little over 5 miles on the pathway, then ride my bike via the dirt roads back to my car for a round trip of about 10 miles. Mountain biking on the pathway is not permitted.

The trail mostly follows the river, although at times you can't see it for the thick forest. It meanders across high banks and through wetlands created by swift-flowing little tributaries feeding the South Branch. You will find several scenic vistas and, at times, you are right down by the river where you can hear it rushing by. Eagles frequently perch in tall trees along the river.

Along the way, you pass a number of access roads coming into the area for anglers, and paths leading down to the river. Some of the more interesting points along the river are noted with trail signposts, which also keep track of your mileage.

Durant's Castle, where I ended my pilgrimage, is an interesting bit of history. An industrialist named Durant built a huge castle on a bluff overlooking the river in the early 1930s. It had just been completed—never lived in—when burned it to the ground. Then, the Great Depression came, and it was never rebuilt. Look closely and you can still see the castle's faint footprint.

Terrell's Trail Notes

🇹 The pathway is well marked with DNR blue triangles and maps at every signpost. Post 2 marks the entrance to Canoe Harbor Campground. Signpost 4—Dogtown—was the site where hunters would gather in the 19th century to hunt game they later sold in the cities. They all had dogs, hence the name of the impromptu community.

🇹 Signpost 5 marks Downey's Place, the site of an exclusive fishing club in the 1920s, still a popular spot for anglers entering the river. Stone stairways lead down to the river. After you cross over Thayer Creek, you reach signpost 8 along the High Banks. There's a bench with a splendid view of the South Branch overlooking a bend in the river.

🇹 Within a half mile, the trail heads back down along the river and comes to signpost 9, the site of Durant's Castle. Follow the side trail down to the river for a breathtaking, close-up view of the Au Sable.

🇹 The pathway is also a single-track groomed during winter for cross country skiing.

7

Highbanks Rollway

a fall view that stretches for miles

One of my favorite go-to places for color viewing isn't an unknown spot. In fact, on nice fall weekends, it can be pretty busy; which is why I visit mid-week.

Highbanks Rollway overlooks the Manistee River valley, offering stunning fall color views of up to 20 miles across the broad valley. Looking down at the forest canopy you'll see a crescendo of colorful hues—crimsons, oranges, and gold—stretching out in front of you as far as the eye can see.

Enjoying the view from the overlook at High Rollway.

Below, the Manistee River forms a classic horseshoe bend before flowing away along the base of the bluff. This is arguably one of the best fall overlooks in northern Michigan. It is also the highest point along this stretch of the Manistee.

The Rollway has been a popular spot with locals for decades—kind of their own secret fall color stash. That all changed when the DNR put up a platform overlook at the site to help protect the fragile riverbank from visitor overuse and gave it the official name Highbanks Rollway. Prior to that it had been known by several names—the Rollaway, Horseshoe Bend, Highbanks Overlook, and Lookout Point were among the more popular. They used to hold weddings at the spot, and gathered for sunrise Easter services if the dirt road leading back was passable and not still snow covered.

Located south of Kingsley on a dead-end dirt road, it wasn't easy to find until it became a designated site. Now with maps and signs, it would be hard to get lost.

The view came about during the lumbering era that took place early in the last century. Lumbermen loved the high bluffs along the Manistee River. This particular location sits a little over 200 feet above the river valley. They would cut the surrounding forest on the land above the river during the winter, and stack the logs along the bluffs in prime locations. In the spring, they would send thousands of logs tumbling down the banks into the river to float downstream to waiting lumber mills. This would scour the bank of vegetation and trees, which even today have sparsely grown back.

The viewing spot, by whatever name it was known, had become popular enough by the late 1900s that the bank was seriously deteriorated. The North Country Trail (NCT)—which covers 4,600 miles between Vermont and North Dakota—also became a reality, passing right by the overlook and bringing more people into the picture.

The DNR stepped in and put up a platform overlook along the bluff. They designated a parking area, and limited access to the bluff with roped-off areas. It has helped to stabilize the area and make it more appealing.

Once you've spent time drinking in that fabulous vista, you can spend some time hiking along the North Country Trail to the east, or the west, along the bluff for more jaw-dropping panoramas. It also gets you away from the crowds, which you will most likely encounter on a nice fall day. Most, however, will walk to the overlook and take a picture—maybe a moment to enjoy it— before heading back to the vehicle.

Terrell's Trail Notes

🎅 Highbanks Rollway is located south of Kingsley. Take Blackman Road south from the village to County Line Road. Turn right (east), and in a few miles, the road curves south, becoming No. 4 Road. At the next curve, a well-traveled dirt road heads left. Follow it to the bluff, where it dead-ends at the overlook parking area. A sign with an NCT map on one side, and information about the area on the other, marks the trail back to the overlook.

🎅 You can hike for a mile or so out and back along the NCT either way from the platform overlook and uncover more wonderful views along the trail. It makes a nice hike away from any crowd.

🎅 You could also, with a friend, spot a car on 29 ½ Road, just above Baxter Bridge where the NCT crosses, and enjoy a scenic 2.4-mile hike from the overlook to the road. It's easiest hiking down to the road.

The other mushroom season

Come early September, it's always amazing to see the color start to spring up on woodland floors. Not up in the trees—I'm talking about the colorful fall mushrooms suddenly taking sprout on the forest floor, stumps, logs, and trees.

September—National Mushroom Month—is a great time to head into the woods in search of the elusive fungi. Springtime hordes of mushroom hunters take to the woods in search of a single variety: the morel. Autumn offers a lot less competition in terms of people and many more edible choices.

There are wonderful varieties of mushrooms available throughout the late summer and fall season in our forests, and many people like eating them more than morels. There are over 4,000 different varieties to sort through, which makes identification critical, because only about 100 are considered edible. Each has its own unique flavor.

An old friend who lived near Lewiston, and a longtime member of the Michigan Mushroom Hunters Club, offered this advice to me:

"First time pickers are best going with someone who knows fall mushrooms and has hunted them. It isn't worth getting poisoned if you don't know what you are doing," he cautioned. "Morels are fairly easy to identify, and that's all you are looking for in the spring. Fall is different, with so many to sort through. If you aren't 110 percent sure about what you are picking, don't eat it.

"Starting out, pick two or three varieties, take them home, and really make sure of the identification," the veteran mushroomer stressed. "Go online and look at several pictures. Find identifying traits to help you feel sure of what you're looking at. In a couple of years, expand your horizons, but don't try to pick too many at the start. You'll only be confused and frustrated."

Here are a few easier to identify fall mushrooms, which are also good to eat. Just go for a hike on any of your favorite woodland trails and keep your eyes open.

SHAGGY MANES are one of the easiest fall mushrooms to identify. The cap is white and sits on a tall, straight stem with a ring low down on the stem. Called the "urban mushroom," young ones—still firm and the cap still attached to stalk—are considered very edible. They don't keep well, though, and should be eaten quickly after picking.

THE CHANTERELLE, with its large yellow-orange, often wavy, irregular cap is fairly easy to spot in the woods. It gives off a pleasant, apricot odor and is prized for its superb flavor.

OYSTER MUSHROOMS, deep bluish-black to pale gray-brown in color, grow in clusters on trees or downed logs. Very edible, they are good in soufflés, soups and chowders, and scrambled eggs. Tear them, instead of slicing, for cooking preparation.

HONEY MUSHROOMS—so named because of their honey-like color—grow in clusters on the ground. They're easy to find, and are considered a delicacy in Europe. They must be well cooked before consumption; if undercooked, they can cause stomach cramps and diarrhea.

HEN-OF-THE-WOODS grow at the base of oak trees. They're large, with semicircular caps fused together. Normally gray to brown in color, they are easy to identify and considered a treat that goes with just about everything.

CHICKEN-OF-THE-WOODS, bright orange and yellow in color, is considered succulent with a mild flavor when it's still young. Older specimens turn a dull yellow and turn brittle.

The Michigan Mushroom Hunter's Club offers seminars on identifying fall mushrooms at various locations throughout the state. You can check the club out at www.michiganmushroomhunters.org.

8

Green Point Dunes

great trails, great views

In 2004, I hiked to the top of a perched dune just south of Elberta with Glen Chown, executive director for the Grand Traverse Regional Land Conservancy (GTRLC), for a view of what was to become Green Point Dunes Nature Preserve. Today it's considered one of the most outstanding views along the Lake Michigan shoreline.

"I call this our *Sound of Music* view," exclaimed Chown at the time.

Between this nature preserve and Arcadia Dunes to the south, the conservancy preserved about 5 miles of undeveloped Lake Michigan shoreline. You'll find sand dunes, secluded beach walks, and, if you're there at dusk, magnificent sunsets over Lake Michigan. Throw in an ancient shipwreck—located just offshore—and add the potential for watching hang gliders floating on thermal currents over lake and dunes. What more could you ask from a nature preserve?

Autumn is one of the best times to visit. Two overlook platforms on top offer panoramic, steal-your-breath views of the shoreline far below. You look across the Lake Herring valley to a distant ridge of forested hills and more tall, rugged-looking perched dunes stretching to the south. Add in the colorful, forested mosaic stretching inland as far as the eye can see. It's fall eye-candy.

The shipwreck, the remains of the *City of Boston*, was a 136-foot-long wooden steamer that sank in a blinding November snowstorm in 1873. It broke up on a sandbar; the crew made it to shore. The ship's remains are in about 8 feet of water, and can be seen when conditions are right from the platform overlook that hangs off the dunes' edge.

The Green Point Flyers Association—a group of hang gliders and paragliders—owns land just north of the preserve where they launch off a platform about 400 feet above the lake. Maybe you'll be lucky enough to catch them in flight.

Terrell's Trail Notes

T The main parking area for the 242-acre preserve—complete with an informative kiosk—is on Green Point Road, off M-22, about 2 miles south of Elberta.

T From the kiosk trailhead, a nearly 3-mile loop trail will take you to two overlooks, plus down to the beach and back up. The first overlook offers Chown's panoramic *Sound of Music* vista. The southerly view looks across Herring Lake and a wide valley to Arcadia Dunes Preserve and Old Baldy, a dune landmark. Trace the gentle curve of the lake stretching south.

T From the first overlook, the trail leads to a perched overlook on the edge of the steep dune face. It offers beautiful views of the shoreline and lake far below. Occasionally, there are Great Lakes freighters heading up or down the lake, and you're often eye level with gulls.

T The trail continues down to a set of stairs that descend the final steep drop to the beach. In 2020, the stairs to the beach were removed because of high water levels. Access to what is left of the beach is strongly discouraged.

T It's about a mile back up to the trailhead. This is a good workout, and also a way to examine the makeup of these massive dunes along the Lake Michigan shoreline.

9

Elberta Dunes

a view from other side

I'm kind of like the bear "that went over the mountain to see what he could see." I'm always wondering what there is on the other side of the hill, or, in Michigan, more likely what's over the dune.

Hiker taking a photo from top of Elberta Dune South.

Having visited the Lake Michigan shoreline-side of the Elberta Dunes for years, I would often wonder what the view would look like from the top of those massive dunes that stretch south as far as the eye can see. In 2010, the Grand Traverse Regional Land Conservancy and the Village of Elberta entered into an agreement to purchase 58 acres just south of the village. The parcel—today called Elberta Dunes South— is located between M-22 and Lake Michigan, and includes a towering dune that rises over 300 feet above the lake and village. It's the backside of those towering dunes you see from the lakeshore.

A single trail leads from the parking area along the highway to the top of the dune. There's a little bit of everything here—a majestic glacial moraine, towering dunes, sweeping views of Lake Michigan, and, looking inland, the untouched forests of the Betsie River Valley.

We have lots of great views scattered around northern Michigan and along the lakeshore, but this is certainly one of the most panoramic. It's almost a 360-degree view. Stretching south are more rugged dunes, rising above the lake. It reminds me of a wild coast. Looking inland to the north, you see the dunes below you and Betsie Bay in the distance. The village of Elberta lies along its southern shore. The Betsie River Valley extends east.

It's not uncommon to see eagles gliding along the coast, often about eye level. This is not a large preserve, but what it offers—including the steal-your-breath view—is so much more. Rare species, such as Pitcher's thistle and Lake Huron locust, call it home. There's a quarter mile of sandy beach that goes with the property, and piping plovers nest along the shoreline. However, it's not easy to get down to the beach; there is no trail and it's a steep climb back up the dune face.

This bear is glad he got to see the other side of the dune. Fall is one of the most beautiful times for a visit, and hunting isn't allowed on the property.

Terrell's Trail Notes

▼ The parking—a large mowed area alongside M-22—is marked with a sign. The trail leads west towards the woods below the dune. It isn't a long hike—a little over a mile round trip—but it is a good vertical climb of over 300 feet to the top. Enter the woods and begin to climb as the trail turns north, reaching a grassy bowl about halfway up. The trail abruptly turns as you come to the bowl, almost doubling back on itself, and begins a steep climb up the side of the dune to reach the top. This part of the trail reminds me of a sandy goat path, and its about as wide. The well-defined trail is easy to follow.

▼ You pop out of the trees above a large, open blowout bowl facing Lake Michigan. Head right just a short distance for some great views of the shoreline far below. Head left for a short, easy climb along the edge of the blowout to panoramic views of the countryside, Betsie Bay, Elberta, and Frankfort. You can trace the Betsie River Valley by heading east, and look down on the parking area where you started. What a fall view, looking out over colorful forests stretching as far as you can see!

Photo: Adobe Stock

Piping plover

Chasing storms along the Lake Michigan coast

When high winds are forecast along the lakeshore, I think of *Tales of Brave Ulysses* by Cream: "the sirens sweetly singing, for the sparkling waves are calling."

A high winds forecast is like a siren call for me. Windstorms can pack a wallop along the Lake Michigan shoreline. When gales hit the coast, the result can be spectacular.

Horizontal sheets of rain, surf crashing on rocks and break walls sending spray several feet in the air, lake foam whipped by the wind—yes, big lake storms that rage from October through December can put on quite a show.

My favorite place to head when winds are high is Elberta and Frankfort. The view from the Elberta scenic overlook above the beach gives you a panoramic view of the piers, breakwaters, and lighthouse.

I quickly discovered after moving here over 40 years ago, that you never take weather for granted up here. The Great Lakes provide their own steering currents, making predictions hard to pinpoint. They seem to suck low pressures right into the vortex and ramp up winds, crossing long stretches of wide-open water.

I got sucked into the vortex of storm-watching at the twin villages years ago. With breakwater piers and the lighthouse in the way of the storm, trying to hold back the menacing waves, it's a stunning sight.

Over the years, I've found others also drawn to the scene. Like moths drawn to a flame, we show up for the spectacle.

One of the worst windstorms I recall hitting the coast was in late October 2010. Wind gusts were reported reaching 70 mph up and down the coast. It was like a lake hurricane. If I remember right, a buoy in the middle of Lake Michigan recorded waves reaching 20 feet.

I drove over and parked up on the Elberta beach scenic overlook. The lake had been whipped to a wind-driven fury, producing a writhing froth. Waves were crashing into the Frankfort harbor breakwater, sending spray almost over the top of the lighthouse.

After bracing myself against my car to keep from swaying in the wind, I took some pictures from the overlook, then decided to drive down to the beach and park. I was going to walk out the boardwalk towards the pier to get a little more up-close and personal with the storm.

Not a good idea.

Without thinking, I parked facing into the wind. I pushed my door open—not easy against the wind. As I stood up, a gust slammed the door back into me, knocking me off my feet and back into the seat. Again, I got the door open and braced myself, pushing against the door as I stood, and was able to hold it open.

Standing there, I remember remarking that the wind was blowing so hard, the sand was stinging my legs through my jeans. People were standing by

another car a few feet away, looking my way and laughing. I then realized that when the door slammed me back into the car, somehow my jeans became unbuckled and were down around my knees.

We all had a good laugh.

A December windstorm can throw in some dramatic icing effects as well. Large waves will coat the pier, breakwaters, and the lighthouse in ice. The lake can look like a giant slushy, as waves rock back and forth. Dress warmly. As gales buffet and lash the shoreline, that icy wind can feel like the sting of a whip.

Seeing the raw power of a wind-driven Lake Michigan whipped into frenzy is a humbling experience. Especially when you're de-pantsed.

10

Palmer Woods

a pleasant fall stroll

The Palmer Woods Forest Reserve offers some nice trail systems that cater to a wide range of forest users.

Hikers and cross country skiers share the same trails, but in the winter, they're groomed with set tracks, specifically for Nordic skiing. With the wide trail system, you can also snowshoe alongside the tracks.

The mountain bike trails are a separate trail system.

What I enjoy most about the Forest Reserve are the peaceful, scenic, picturesque strolls along the Price Valley Trail, especially in the fall. I call it a stroll because it's almost like walking along a boulevard through the forest. It's a nice, wide two-track that goes from the Palmer Woods' trailhead off Wheeler Road, almost 2 miles to an access off Darwin Road. Darwin Road is seasonal and not plowed in winter.

The Palmer family, who owned the land for many years, operated the land in sustainable fashion as a working forest, growing and harvesting the timber to keep the forest healthy. The old logging roads have turned into hiking and skiing trails, and the forest is beautiful.

The Price Valley Trail quickly heads down into a fairly long valley with tall ridges on the right. These house the Loop Trail, with the mountain biking trails on top. It's a pleasant walk through the woods on this wide pathway. There are many colorful pockets of trees scattered all along the trail. Many large trees—primarily colorful beech and maple—are sprinkled throughout the forest.

With a friend, you could spot a vehicle at the Darwin Road entrance and leave the other vehicle at the trailhead. That's about a 2-mile hike one way, with a moderate climb over the last half mile up to Darwin Road.

The reserve has been adding new trails almost every year, but this remains my favorite hike in the Palmer Woods.

Kudos to the Leelanau Conservancy and the Palmer family who worked together to preserve this beautiful forest for all of us to enjoy.

Terrell's Trail Notes

❚ Darwin Road leads off Wheeler Road, about 2 miles north of the trailhead parking, and it's about a 1.5 miles more up to post 9, back off the road. That's where you leave a car if you are doing a one-way hike with a friend. The trails are well marked, easy to follow, and detailed maps appear at each signpost. An out-and-back hike along Price Valley to Darwin Road is a little under 4 miles.

❚ You can also do a 2-mile hike—out and back—from the trailhead parking lot and skip Darwin Road. Hike from post 1 to post 6 along the Price Valley Trail. It's about a mile between the trailhead and post 6.

❚ Add a scenic half mile by hiking from post 4, up to 5, on your way to post 6. It's not a difficult climb. As you hike from 5 to 6, take a look at the tall ridge looming above you. At times you almost feel like you are in the Appalachian foothills. Return to the parking area along the valley floor to post 4. The only out-and-back portion of the hike will be between posts 1 and 4.

❚ However you choose to explore Price Valley Trail, you won't be disappointed. It's a very pleasant stroll in Dr. Palmer's forest.

11

Miller Creek

a scenic delight to hike

Miller Creek Nature Reserve offers one of the most delightful, scenic trail systems in the Traverse City area—that most people haven't heard of.

Located below the Grand Traverse Crossings Mall, it's in an unlikely area to even look for a hiking trail.

A light snow along Miller Creek.

A large wooded valley with streams, a marsh, and meadows sits below the ridge behind the mall between South Airport Road and Cass Road. Arbors Apartments are on the other side of the valley. There are two 1-mile loops, a .75-mile loop, and a .5-mile out-and-back trail for a total of over 3 miles of wonderful hiking. Several hundred feet of boardwalks cross the marshland.

There are red pine plantations, a beech forest, cedar swamps, and plenty of nature to watch. I've seen hawks flying over the valley and deer browsing in the meadows and swamps.

The best trailhead for entering the valley is located behind Aldi's discount grocery store off of South Airport Road. A portion of the trail leads over to Sabin School, coming out right behind it. Eventual plans call for linking the Miller Creek Reserve trail with the Boardman Valley Nature Preserve via a connection across Cass Road and through an easement on the Sabin School property, according to the Grand Traverse Conservation District.

It's a nice scenic hike around the valley, and once you're down in the valley, you won't even notice that the busy Crossing Mall, with all the hubbub and noise, sits just above you. It's an urban park in the midst of all the development; an oasis for you, the animals, and birds. Fall is beautiful here, and winter makes for a nice snowshoe trek.

Terrell's Trail Notes

T Behind Aldi's, head down a quick path to a trail intersection and a bench along Miller Creek, a tributary for the Boardman River. Once you cross the creek, the trail splits, with one section leading across the open area and another spur heading left following the creek.

T Head across the meadow-like area, which can be wet in spring and summer. Fall is the best time to access the valley. Once you cross the open area, you come to a pond and a bench. Continue on a trail behind the bench, crossing more open field before coming to a small creek you hop over. On the other side, the trail becomes more pronounced. Follow it to the left. The Arbors Apartments sit along a ridge above the trail on the right—mostly unnoticeable—and a marsh is on the left.

T Another trail sign soon intersects. You can head left across a boardwalk through a swampy area—that you have to take eventually. But first, I like to follow the trail right through woods below the condominiums. It leads to another long boardwalk, crossing more cedar swamp, and it comes out behind Sabin School. It's a mile out and back from the intersection to Sabin—plus the return to the split—but well worth it. The boardwalk section is a good place for wildlife viewing.

T When you return to the split, proceed straight ahead across the boardwalk, heading through more cedar swamp. A dirt path leads the .75-mile back to Miller Creek. Return to the trailhead behind Aldi by following the trails left on either side of the creek. You can, however, head right and follow the scenic trail for about a half a mile, out and back along the creek as it rushes to meet the Boardman River, before heading back to the trailhead.

12

Pelizzari Natural Area

a natural fit

This small, 62-acre natural area located at the base of Old Mission Peninsula is today one of the more popular hiking areas adjacent to Traverse City. In winter, the trails are home to snowshoers and cross country skiers.

There are around 3 miles of trails that flow around an old orchard and remnant farm fields, through upland hardwood forests and a section of old-growth hemlock forest above East Shore Drive and East Bay.

My favorite time of year to hike it is autumn. Fall colors, with all the hardwood trees, can be blazing, especially as you walk around the lower meadow area. The edges of the upper field also provide good color viewing.

The hardwoods, and what they call Middle Woods, are about a quarter mile from the parking area located on busy Center Road (M-37).

I was amazed the first time I hiked it during summer. I went from hearing cars speeding up Center Road to occasionally hearing speed boats buzzing up and down East Bay as I hiked along trails through the old-growth hemlock forest. Once you leave the open orchard land at the beginning of the hike, you are mostly immersed in woods and beautiful meadows.

Gene Pelizzari owned the orchard and farm that had been in his family since the 1920s. He quit working the land in the late 1980s, but wanted to see it preserved as a natural area for future generations to enjoy. With the assistance of nearby neighbors like Dave Murphy and Mary Van Valin, the Grand Traverse Regional Land Conservancy and Peninsula Township worked together to place a township millage proposal on the ballot in 2008 to purchase the land and create Pelizzari Natural Area.

"It's been a real boon to area residents throughout the Traverse City area," exclaimed Murphy when I spoke with him. "It's so close to so many people who can enjoy a quick outing year-round. In just a few minutes, you can be off in a wonderful natural area away from the distractions of our busy, connected world."

Terrell's Trail Notes

🇹 There are maps and numbered posts at all trail intersections.

🇹 Hike up through the old orchard field from the parking lot to post 1, where you'll enter the natural area's hardwood forest. The trail begins with a long descent along a ravine, past post 2 to post 3. Continue on to post 5 as you hike the edge of the lower meadow. A loop trail goes through the old-growth hemlock forest and along a bluff above East Shore Road. You can see the bay through the trees.

🇹 Once you return to post 5, head over to posts 6 and 7 for a pleasant hike through the lower meadow. Before returning to the parking lot—which can be done by hiking up to post 11—walk up to the bench on the hill on the way over to post 8: It offers a stunning view of the meadow and trails. During color season, it's a great place to linger and enjoy the view.

🇹 Continue to the upper field. Fall colors can also be dazzling along the edges of the field, and you can get a good glimpse of East Bay through the trees along the east side of the trail. Heading back to the parking lot, the trail continues to hug the lower meadow as you proceed to posts 11, 12, and 13, with a good climb back through the Middle Woods section. A bench is positioned just beyond post 13 that offers a nice view of the old orchard field, and it's a good place to rest after the climb before returning to the trailhead.

13

Yuba Creek

a fall smorgasbord

On a drive looking for scenic locations, you're always anticipating what's just around the corner or over the ridge. Sometimes it can literally be just over a ridge, close to home.

Hundreds of vehicles pass by the beautiful Yuba Creek Natural Area, just over a ridge off U.S. 31 between Acme and Elk Rapids, and most people are unaware of the long, scenic valley and hiking trails. One of the trailheads is located off the busy highway on top of the hill before it plunges down by the old Yuba school, but I rarely see cars parked there.

An old beech tree at Yuba Creek.

Fall is stunning in the valley when viewed from the top of the ridge where trails lead you to jaw-dropping overlooks. The 413-acre preserve, purchased by Acme Township and the Grand Traverse Regional Land Conservancy (GTRLC) in 2002, features the namesake creek that flows the length of the valley, a mix of wetlands along the creek, open meadows, and upland hardwood forests. It helps protect the East Bay watershed.

Unfortunately, you can't see the creek anymore. The GTRLC website claims you can observe nesting eagles in the area, which you apparently could when the preserve first opened. Not today. You can frequently spot deer moving through the valley and hawks patrolling above the open meadow, looking for easy prey. It's also home to otter and mink.

The best trailhead for exploring the valley is located off Yuba Road. It offers a nice trail up the long valley and spur trails that lead to scenic overlooks along the ridge, including the overlook from the trailhead off U.S. 31. From the overlooks—especially the one that's accessed from the end of the valley trail—look across the valley to distant hills on the other side, some containing orchards that light up in the spring with white blossoms. To the south are more faraway hills that create a colorful mosaic in the fall.

I like visiting the preserve in spring and fall, both beautiful times of the year that seem to highlight what the area has to offer: invigorating hikes, drop-dead overlook views, and serenity. On most of my visits, I run into few other hikers. As you hike up the valley, enjoy the beauty of the preserve, and the peace and quiet. Even though a busy highway is just over the long ridge, you thankfully hear no traffic noise.

Terrell's Trail Notes

🚩 The trailhead on U.S. 31 provides a short half-mile round trip. The trailhead on Yuba Road provides better trails, more distance, and more scenic views. Hiking the main, out-and-back valley trail and spurs leading to scenic ridge views will net you close to 4.5 miles.

14

Jordan River

**a popular river float
for all seasons**

Looking for a short, scenic river
to float—one that's a little bit
feisty to keep things interesting?

I've got just the river for you.

The Jordan River, Michigan's
first designated Wild and
Scenic Natural River, is a short,
beautiful river that receives
high marks for both fishing
and paddling. It's considered
one of the state's finest trout
fishing streams, and many float
enthusiasts consider it one of
our premier paddling streams.

The 24-mile river itself is not long by river standards, and the navigable portion—most of it in Antrim County—is only a little over 10 miles. The first put-in is at Graves Crossing, and you can float the river all the way to Lake Charlevoix and East Jordan. Most people take out at Rogers Road bridge—a little under a 9-mile float. For the last mile and a half to the lake, you're basically paddling through a marsh. Not very scenic and quite slow.

The upper river tumbles and flows through a beautiful, heavily forested valley. It's very scenic, with lots of aspen, birch, and maple throughout the forest. You see a few cabins, but not many. Cedars line the banks along the upper stretches of river, keeping it cool even on hot summer days. The short length makes it perfect for a morning or afternoon float. It's also one of the few north-flowing rivers in the Lower Peninsula.

A warm fall day is one of the best times to enjoy a paddle. You may have it all to yourself. Summer can sometimes be chaotic with all the paddlers and tubers.

The Jordan is known for its clarity of water, according to outdoor author Jerry Dennis. In his book, *Canoeing Michigan Rivers*, he says it has the purest water of any Lower Peninsula river.

Terrell's River Trail Notes

🛶 It's about a 3-hour paddle, with takeouts and put-ins spaced about an hour apart. The first section of river from Graves Crossings is narrow. You need to be able to maneuver your canoe or kayak through tight corners and overhanging trees and branches. That first hour is considered one of the more challenging paddles in northern Lower Michigan. Novice paddlers often dump here. They should consider putting in at Old State Road bridge, which is around a 2-hour paddle to Rogers Road bridge.

🛶 Taking off from the Graves Crossing access, you immediately get into the heart and character of the Jordan. Within the first .1 miles, tight bends, a swift-flowing current, and riffles compete with some standing waves.

🛶 The river remains winding and moderately quick through the next couple of takeouts to Rogers Road, but is somewhat easier to paddle. No noise, no rush—just you and the river and the rhythmic sound of the paddle dipping into the water. On a hot, summer day when the beach is crowded and the lake noisy with the sound of powerboats and jet skis, head for the cool, quiet Jordan River. It may not take you to the promised land, but it will rejuvenate your soul.

🛶 Two liveries—Swiss Hideaway at Graves Crossing and Jordan Valley Outfitters in East Jordan—service the Jordan River. The road crossings are set up so that each is about an hour below the other, and you can do floats of one-, two- and three-hours. Both liveries rent kayaks, canoes, and tubes. Jordan Valley Outfitters also offers raft rides and guided tours, as well as popular winter rafting trips.

🛶 Both liveries also offer car spotting for those who have their own equipment. For more information on Jordan Valley Outfitters, you can log onto www.jvoutfitters.com; and for Swiss Hideaway, log onto www.jordanriverfun.com.

15

Jordan River Valley

some of the best fall views in Lower Michigan

Fall comes early to the Jordan River Valley. It's one of the spots in our neck of the woods that turns quickly, offering outstanding fall views from ridges flanking the 12-mile valley. By the end of September, weekends will be busy with "leaf peepers" craning for that view. Midweek is not as bad.

Deadman's Hill Overlook

The Valley is an 18,000-acre block within the Mackinaw State Forest. You can access it via the Jordan River Road and Penney Bridge Road—both dirt—or the 19-mile Jordan River Pathway. Also, a portion of the North Country Trail (NCT) that stretches from Vermont to North Dakota runs through the Valley. Best of all, the entire valley is completely free of development. The river was Michigan's first waterway to be officially designated as a Wild and Scenic River by the federal government.

Taking the Jordan River Road that exits off U.S. 131, just north of the turnoff for Deadman's Hill Overlook and Penney Bridge Road, you'll get an eye-level look at the scenic valley. The dirt roads parallel the river much of the way. Penney Bridge Road exits on to M-66 at the other end. Along the way, you pass the Penney Bridge parking area—a great place for a quick hike and pictures.

There are two overlooks that you can drive to: Deadman's Hill, off U.S. 131 north of Alba; and Landslide, off Alba Highway and Harvey Road. Both overlooks involve short, easy walks to amazing views. Autumn reds and yellows spread like a wildfire across the valley and up distant ridges. The sweeping vistas stretch as far as the eye can see. Both arguably offer some of the best fall views in northern Michigan.

Deadman's Hill Overlook—high on a ridge, 435 feet above the valley—is named for a young lumberjack who tragically lost his life in 1910 while trying to transport an overloaded Big Wheel filled with cut trees down to the valley floor and river.

Terrell's Trail Notes

🐾 The Jordan River Pathway is one of the most popular backpacking trails in the Lower Peninsula, with more than 3,000 hikers making the trek annually. It is not an easy walk. It's rugged, with constant climbs up and down the ridgelines. The pathway begins at Deadman's Hill. A rustic, walk-in campground at Penney Bridge—at the other end of the valley—splits the 19-mile trek almost down the middle. A quick, marked detour on the return trip will take you to the Jordan River Fish Hatchery. There is no camping permitted along the pathway except for that one, designated site.

🐾 A short 3-mile hike—which doesn't go to the river—is also available, starting from Deadman's Hill. It goes down into the valley, crossing several springs that feed the river, and back up, allowing you to experience the deep forest. Just remember—it's a long uphill climb to get back to the overlook.

🐾 Parking at Penney Bridge allows you to cross the river and walk about a half a mile up to the rustic campground. Continue on the pathway for another half mile, and you climb to a wooden bench along a ridge above the river—more nice valley views. The total hike is 2 miles, round trip. The camp site was a former logging camp. It was established about a century ago, and later, in the 1930s, became a CCC camp.

🐾 At Landside Overlook, the main attraction is the view. It's a short walk from the parking area. The Jordan River Pathway passes through.

A century ago the valley was just a sea of stumps. Today it is lush, beautiful, and well worth a visit, especially in the fall.

16

Avalanche Preserve

avoid the crush of fall leaf peepers

Fall in northern Michigan sometimes reminds me of the zombie apocalypse. Leaf-peeping tourists are everywhere; eyes fixed on the horizon, blinded by dazzling bursts of woodland color, they amble by with transfixed stares.

The key is to seek lesser known or more difficult overlooks offering stellar fall views. One of my favorites qualifies on both points: Avalanche Preserve. It's a former ski hill that towers over Boyne City. The overlook rises well over 400 feet above the village, and the 462 steps it takes to climb to the top discourage many seeking easier access to fall panoramas. I've encountered few people over the years enjoying this vista.

The panoramic view is worth the long climb. You overlook Boyne City, nestled along the Lake Charlevoix shoreline far below you. The view stretches the full length of the large lake. On a sunny day, catch a glint off Lake Michigan on the far horizon. The ridges and hills surrounding Lake Charlevoix will be splashed with colors, offset by the steely-blue lake waters. It's one of the best views in Lower Michigan any time of year, but exceptional in fall with the surrounding hardwood hills aglow.

The tall, steep ridge was home to a downhill ski area in the 1950s. Called Avalanche Peak, it had rope tows, a poma lift, and even a double chairlift operating before closing in the 1960s. The open slopes that still exist are popular for sledding in the winter. It's now part of the Boyne City park program.

There are two, very nice platform overlooks complete with benches and a water fountain with an attached tray at the bottom for your dog. A nice touch—it's a big climb for them as well.

Terrell's Trail Notes

▼ There are about 7 miles of trails across the ridge available for hikers, mountain bikers, cross country skiers, and snowshoers. The hike I like is about 2.5 miles, which is plenty for me, considering the climb to the top.

▼ The parking lot for the preserve is located on the southeast side of the village, off Lake Street. It's hard to miss the towering hill. There's a lodge with restrooms located near the parking lot. The steps go up the right side of the hill, and start just beyond the parking lot for hikers.

▼ The top of the hill is a little over 1,000 feet above sea level, offering wonderful panoramic views. You'll feel like you are on top of Charlevoix County. The hike up adds to that feeling—it's a good climb. Pick a sunny, warm fall day, pack a lunch, and don't forget the camera. I like to spend an hour or so drinking in that wonderful view. It's the reward for the hike up there.

▼ Once you're ready to head back down, there are a couple of options. You could go back down the steps, or you can follow the main trail across the top of the ridge that winds through the colorful forest back down to the parking lot. That's my preference.

▼ The main trail goes along the ridge, drops through the thick forest, and wanders along the bottom of the ridge and back to the parking area. You will have the trail to yourself most of the time. There are some views off the backside of the hill looking out over more valleys and distant hills, but nothing like the front-side views. It's a nice "woodsy" trail.

▼ There's also a separate mountain bike trail—over 7 miles—that takes you to the top and back down. It's for expert riders.

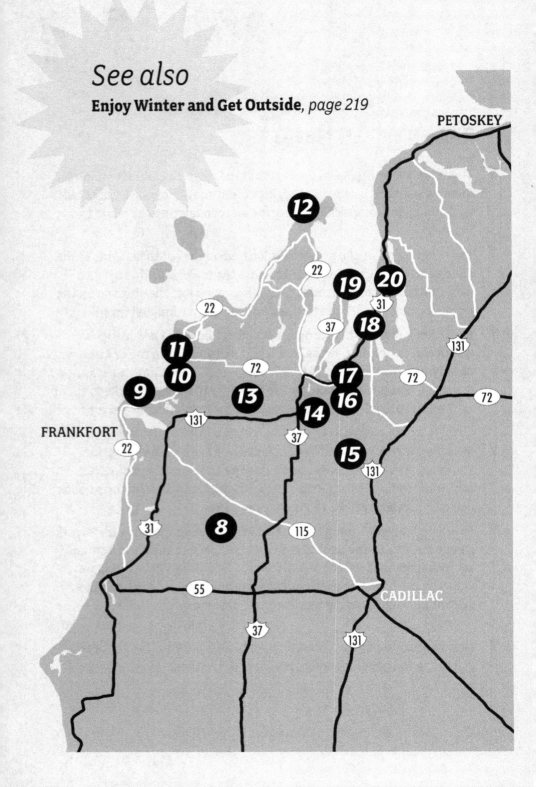

See also
Enjoy Winter and Get Outside, *page 219*

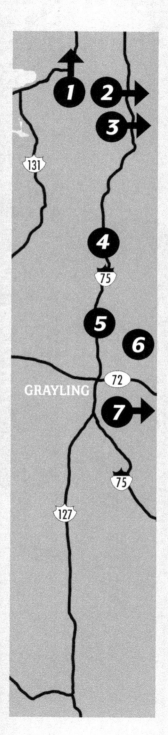

Winter

Enjoy winter and get outside

That old saying, "cabin fever is a preventable disease," is true. Getting outside for a hike—if there's lack of snow—or snowshoeing and cross country skiing—when snow finally arrives—will do wonders for your psyche.

Snowshoeing is the easiest way to explore our woodlands, and there are numerous trails to investigate and enjoy. What people seem to often forget is that winter hiking is also an option when there's a lack of snow. There are so many options to getting out and enjoying winter activities.

But, what if you haven't had an opportunity to give snowshoeing or cross country skiing a try? There's a cure for that too.

Winter Trails Day normally takes place the first or second Saturday in January at a handful of locations around our area. It offers children and adults new to snow sports a chance to try snowshoeing and/or cross country skiing for free.

In the past, the event has been held at Timber Ridge Resort in conjunction with TART Trails; Cross Country Ski Headquarters in Roscommon; and Crystal Mountain, Boyne Mountain, and Boyne Highlands. Hundreds of people have been introduced to the liberating feeling of getting out on a pair of skis or snowshoes during winter thanks to this annual event.

The event was not held in 2021 due to Covid. Hopefully, it will return in 2022 and become an annual event again. It had been held ten years in a row prior to the pandemic-related cancellation.

The most difficult aspect of snowshoeing used to be putting them on with all the straps, but new step-in models have made it much easier. Snowshoeing is very much like walking, and after a few steps, you will have it down.

Cross country skiing is a little more involved than learning to snowshoe. With the short lesson you get at Winter Trails Day, most people learn the basics in one session.

Many people never get beyond shuffling around on skis, much like walking. But they still have a great time, get some exercise, and enjoy the outdoors. Those looking for a more rugged workout can get that by varying the terrain and intensity of the outing.

Terrell's Trail Notes

▼ Around the city you will find trails to snowshoe at Grand Traverse Natural Education Reserve, Grand Traverse Commons, and Hickory Meadows.

▼ On Old Mission Peninsula, the Pelizzari Natural Area at the base of the peninsula, and Lighthouse Park at the tip, offer scenic trails for snowshoe hikes.

▼ Nearby Grass River Natural Area in Antrim County offers several miles of trails and boardwalks along the river and through nearby bogs and uplands.

▼ Brown Bridge Quiet Area, near Ranch Rudolf, has scenic trails along the ridges above the Boardman River valley.

▼ None of these snowshoe hikes are difficult, and you can vary the length as you wish.

1

Munising

a wonderland of frozen waterfalls and ice caves

Over the 40-some years I've lived up here, I've made several trips to Munising in the UP. It's one of my favorite all-season outdoor communities, especially in winter.

The area is home to two of the UP's best groomed cross country tail systems: Valley Spur and Pictured Rocks. In addition, I really enjoy the number of wintertime attractions that are fairly accessible in the backcountry.

Well-trodden trails lead to beautiful frozen waterfalls, ice caves, and pillars of ice formed by water dripping down sandstone cliffs. These are some of the most unusual natural attractions found around the Great Lakes. March is normally a great time of year to visit as the temperatures are warmer, the days longer, and the ice formations have had all winter to build up.

The two easiest waterfalls to reach are both near the village. Munising Falls is located at Pictured Rocks Visitor Center, and Wagner Falls is just outside town, off M-94.

The Park Service even snow blows the pathway to a viewing platform at Munising Falls where an amazing column of ice drops some 50 feet into a horseshoe-shaped canyon of multicolored rocks, ice, and snow. A late afternoon sun creates some spectacular colors.

Wagner Falls is a short snowshoe hike—a half a mile round trip—to a small fall that cascades down a 100-foot stretch of rock, forming a picturesque setting of ice, rock, and rushing water. A series of platforms and steps along the falls offers close-up views.

Miners Falls is located east of Munising and within the Pictured Rocks National Lakeshore. It's off the road leading back to Miners Castle—an impressive rock formation along the Superior lakeshore. The road to the castle is only partially plowed, so you must park at the end of the plowing and proceed on snowshoes. The trail along the ridge that leads to the falls is marked. It's about a 5-mile round trip, often well trekked, and offers some distant views of Lake Superior. Miners Falls drops about 40 feet into a horseshoe-shaped canyon, and the mist creates dazzling ice formations along the canyon's rock walls. A viewing platform provides breathtaking views.

Laughing Whitefish Falls, located north of Sundell off M-94, drops 100 feet down a series of rock ledges into a deep gorge of layered limestone, giving the falls a rainbow of hued colors. The road back to the falls is not plowed, but often trekked. Park at the entrance and snowshoe or cross country ski to the viewing platform—about a 3 mile round trip.
Steps lead to the bottom of the falls.

A trip to the Eben Ice Caves is always a must. Summer's modest trickle of cedar swamp water down sandstone cliffs becomes huge columns of ice in winter, forming caves with chambers you can walk through. The surface of the cave is smooth, clear, and cold. Curtains and veils formed by the ice columns are chillingly beautiful. The winter sun filters through, illuminating the caves in a cold, blue light. It's not a hard trek, but be careful dropping into the gorge.

The caves are about 4 miles north of the tiny hamlet of Eben, off M-94, on a dead-end road. A sign marks the spot where you can take off across an open field. The path is normally well trodden. Enter the woods on the other side of the field, go around a gate, and it's about a mile back to the caves.

If Munising Bay has solidly frozen over, you can cross the ice from Sandpoint, near Pictured Rocks Visitor Center, to Grand Island, where massive columns of ice form along cliffs. It's about a mile across the open bay to the cliff side of the island. Just verify that the ice is safe. I always look for snowmobile traffic and speak with the people ice fishing.

Munising is our own version of *Frozen*.

2

Black Mountain Forest

remote and scenic

Thoreau said, "The mere existence of wilderness refreshes us."

Take a trip to Black Mountain Forest Recreation Area—located southeast of Cheboygan—and you instantly understand what Thoreau meant. As I pulled away from the area after a couple days of midweek cross country skiing, my body felt tired, but my soul was refreshed and uplifted by the time spent there.

The snow was in great shape, and fresh grooming had set the pathway to near perfection. I saw a few deer throughout the afternoon, and even an eagle soaring high overhead. Despite several cars in the parking lot, I had the trails mostly to myself.

Black Mountain Forest Recreation Area opened in 1994, and now offers close to 30 miles of groomed cross country trails. Some classic-only, but many miles also include skating lanes. A volunteer group has been handling the grooming since 2009 when the DNR stepped aside.

"It's been a big plus to tourism on our side of the state. We have no downhill areas over here, but great cross country skiing," enthused Dennis Paul, a Cheboygan veterinarian who has helped organize the volunteer effort. "We have volunteers and grooming equipment in place."

The area itself was created around 11,000 years ago as the last glaciers retreated north, leaving behind mounds of glacial debris called moraines. Looming over the east side of Black Lake—home to prehistoric sturgeon—the long ridge parallels Lake Huron's shoreline. Serpentine ridges stretch through transition forests of pine and hardwoods, punctuated by spring-fed lakes and populated by wildlife.

The remote area has few signs of civilization. And fortunately, it never will. Michigan's Natural Resources Trust Fund stepped in during the late 1980s and purchased about 9,000 acres of this striking landscape, designating it as a recreation area. Part of it was once a privately owned downhill ski area called Black Mountain, open during the 1960s. The ski area's open slopes are now part of a snowmobile/ORV staging area to access a separate network of trails bisecting the mountain.

Terrell's Trail Notes

🚩 Black Mountain is divided into two quadrants, with Black Mountain Road as the dividing line. The northwest portion contains the most challenging trails, while the northeastern quadrant holds mostly intermediate- and beginner-level trails. Trails on the west side of the road offer a nice mix—from easy kick-and-glide along the mountain spine to a fall line that plunges down the flank with steep climbs back to the top. Three trailheads are scattered around the bottom of the moraine, plus one on top off Black Mountain Road.

🚩 The eastern end trailhead, off CR 489, is where I started at signpost 1. I skied my way up the ridge along well-marked trails. You never go more than a mile without crossing a signpost with numbers, arrows pointing to the next post, and a map.

🚩 Climbing the ridgeline, you'll find overlooks between signposts 6 and 8 that allow brief glimpses of Lake Huron's steely-blue waters—about 6 miles away—shimmering in the distance. The trail climbs gently through woods reaching a shelter and perfect snack stop at post 12.

🚩 The shelter is one of two the DNR constructed along the 30-mile trail system. Three-sided, they are open on one side facing grills and a firepit. Set to block strong north winds, they are quite snug on a cold, windy day. I could see a bonfire here on a moonlit night.

🚩 One of my favorite sections of trail flows along the ridge on the west side of Black Mountain Road. It follows the ridgeline from the top, down to the trailhead on Twin Lakes Road, the northernmost trailhead. Covering about 3 miles, and slightly downhill much of the way, it's a blast to ski. Through the trees you catch glimpses of the huge white expanse of frozen Black Lake paralleling the west side of the mountain.

🚩 Black Mountain Lodge, located adjacent to Twin Lakes trailhead, offers a nice place to stay if you wanted to spend a night to ski all the trails. The trailhead is right across the road.

3

Sturgeon River

cold and beautiful

Those who enjoy the beauty of our Michigan rivers in the summertime—and who doesn't?—might want to consider doing so in winter as well.

Yes, it can be cold. No, make that damn cold, especially when it's barely above zero.

A few years ago, during the first week of January, a group of friends and I decided to go winter rafting on the Sturgeon River. I was looking forward to the experience, but knew I needed to dress warmly. Probably over-warmly because I was going to be sitting for over an hour in a raft on a cold river. The actual air temperature was four degrees during our float.

I wore thermal long underwear under my downhill ski outfit, my Sorel boots, ski hat, and a warm mask to breathe through. Looking much like a large, colorful Pillsbury dough boy—as one of my companions called me—was all right, comfortable enough through most of the trip. Dressing in layers is the key. Despite being cased in thermal socks and boots, however, my feet were cold by trip's end.

The charm and winter quietude of our region became quickly evident during the rafting trip. For our group, the sheer beauty of the trip quickly quelled conversation. After much chatting, laughter, and lots of awed exclamations at the start of our float, we became quieter, understanding the beauty of a winter float trip.

The silence was deep and golden as we glided along, at times passing under overhanging snow-covered cedar branches.

The only sound was the gurgle of rushing water sweeping down the river and around logjams on river bends. We avoided the shelves of ice that sometimes form around sweeping bends, but the river was never frozen completely across. The large rubber raft bounced and worked its way through the sweepers and around obstacles with incredible ease.

Terrell's Trail Notes

T We made the guided trip with Big Bear Adventures in Indian River. They offer 1.5-hour raft trips on the Sturgeon all winter long, seven days a week. All trips are with guides in large rafts that can carry up to six, plus the guide. The guide does the bulk of the steering, although you are given paddles to occasionally help weave the raft around a bend, an ice shelf, or logs. Call 231-238-8181 to schedule a trip or log on to https://bigbearadventures.com.

T Our river guide, longtime Big Bear employee Sean Boughner, was knowledgeable about the river.

"I never get tired of the winter river trips. It's one of my favorite times on the Sturgeon. The beauty, peace, and quiet this time of year is extra-special. You see a lot more wildlife because you can see farther into the woods, and the snow highlights movement," Boughner enthused. "Deer are frequent visitors to the riverbank in a typical winter, and other animals as well because of the open water. Eagles are often seen perched high in big trees along the river, drawn by the prey frequenting the river."

As if on cue, shortly after his discourse, we spotted three deer heading up a ridge trail after a river visit.

4

Gaylord Pathways

a cross country mecca

Located just a snowball throw off I-75, Gaylord is one of the best cross country communities in the Lower Peninsula. The village has a charming alpine motif that would fit right into the Swiss Alps, and there are close to 60 miles of nearby trails, both tracked and untracked, to choose from.

Near town, there are a couple of groomed trails that offer fairly easy skiing.

Thanks to the Gaylord Area Convention & Tourism Bureau for the photo.

It's impossible to not see elk at Aspen Park, only four blocks from downtown and adjacent to the city elk pen. It contains a herd of more than 30 elk—magnificent, large animals crowned with a large antler rack. You're almost guaranteed an up-close and personal look. In case they aren't near the trails, drive over to where the city feeds them at the nearby corner of Grandview and Elkview Roads. The park contains about 2 miles of single-tracked trails, and it's lit for night skiing. Trails glide gently through a hemlock forest.

Pine Baron Pathway offers a little over 6 miles of fairly easy gliding through mixed pine and hardwood forest. It's located about 5 miles west of the city, off Old Alba Road on Lone Pine Road.

There are 3 loops—each about 2 miles in length—that you can mix and match. The outside distance around the loops is 6.2 miles. You'll pass an old, abandoned homestead dating back to the 1930s. The trails are groomed for double-track skiing.

There are two other nearby state-land pathways where you have a chance of seeing elk in the wild.

Shingle Mill Pathway, located about 20 minutes north of Gaylord in the Pigeon River Country State Forest, is a rugged land of contrasts in both terrain and weather. Both the highest and lowest temperature recorded in the Wolverine State has occurred here; from a bone-chilling -51 degrees to a sultry high of 112. The average mean temperature is a chilly 42. Winter is arguably the Pigeon's longest season.

Located about 11 miles east of Vanderbilt, off I-75, the pathway is surrounded by the 106,000-acre Pigeon River Country State Forest and offers trails broken into loops of 1 mile up to 10 miles. There is a .75-mile loop, but I can't picture anybody driving to the Pigeon for something this short.

The pathway is untracked and meanders along the swift-flowing Pigeon River, then climbs into highlands overlooking the river valley. Along the way you pass small, frozen lakes, some with beaver lodges.

Trails start in the back of the state forest campground—you'll come to the campground right after crossing the Pigeon River, heading east from Vanderbilt. I've seen elk while cross country skiing here.

Buttles Road Pathway is located about a half an hour east of Gaylord, off M-72 on Buttles Road. The state-land trail is ungroomed, but sometimes has skied-in tracks.

This pathway offers three loops totaling a little over 6 miles. The most challenging terrain is the last loop, which skirts a couple of small scenic lakes on the back portion. The terrain is rolling, with small forested hills. It's definitely out in the middle of nowhere, but that's what makes it so appealing. I have not seen elk here, but have come across hoofprints on the pathway. Locals say they hang around the area in the winter.

If you decide to spend the night to sample the various trails, there's an abundance of lodging choices—from resorts to quaint "mom and pop" motels—along with a wide variety of restaurants. There's something to fit just about every budget and ski appetite.

5

Forbush Corners

**a cross country trail
adds snowmaking**

Forbush Corners, opened by
Dave Forbush in the mid-1980s
on an old family homestead,
quickly became the unofficial
epicenter of cross country skiing
in northern Michigan.

Dave was passionate about the
sport. He purchased some of
the best grooming equipment
available—which he sometimes
brought to Traverse City to
help with the Vasa race trail
grooming. But that was back
in the early days, when the
Vasa race was held without a
permanent dedicated track.

Forbush Corners was an early skier's paradise—from the ski shop to the warming area and waxing room, and, of course, the well laid-out trail system with both deep tracks and skating lanes on all trails. Dave's off-season was getting ready for the next winter season.

It was devastating to the cross country community when he passed away from cancer in 2014, after a short battle. The good news was that he had thought ahead, laying out the groundwork to keep his beloved Forbush Corners going for future generations. He passed on the touring center to five friends he knew who had the same passion: Ann Wagar, Howard Hansen, Todd Hubbard, Larry Damic, and Mario Kennedy. They all had worked closely with Dave in establishing Forbush Corners and were committed to keeping it going.

The group has made improvements, like adding snowmaking— through a generous donation from a longtime patron—on about 2 kilometers of trail, which allows them to open for groomed cross country skiing in mid-November, well ahead of the rest of northern Michigan's touring centers. It is the only touring center around the Great Lakes with this amount of snowmaking.

Forbush has become a nonprofit, according to Wagar, which will allow them to apply for grant applications to make further improvements down the road. "We've added a new trail called the Freeway Loop, and reopened the Pines Loop. We also reworked a couple of trails to provide more intermediate loops, and, continuing Dave's passion for beautifully groomed trails, we added another Piston Bully 100 to our fleet of groomers," she enthused as we talked about touring center improvements.

Forbush Corners still has the same vibe it had when Dave was alive and overseeing the touring center. It's good to see that passion is still there. It's in good hands and the future looks very promising.

Terrell's Trail Notes

- Forbush Corners is located just east of I-75, about 8 miles north of Grayling on CR 612.

- There's close to 30 kilometers of groomed trail, and if that's not enough, you can access the Weary Legs Trail that's part of the Hartwick Pines State Park with a 7.5-mile groomed cross country system. Lots of miles are available, and all groomed.

- The Flatlands Trail leads to all other trails as it departs the day lodge. It's also the snowmaking trail and lit for night skiing. The easiest trails are the Pancake and Green trails, right off the day lodge, each about 5 kilometers long. If you want difficult, try Lil Stinker and Screamer on the west side. The Back 40 is 5 kilometers of up-and-down trail—a good workout on screaming downhills that won't scare you. You also connect with the Hartwick Pines trail system from these west side trails.

- If you want thrills and plenty of hills, head over to the east side trails and tackle Rollercoaster—everything the name implies—and Badlands. Lil Coaster is a miniature version of those two. There's close to 20 kilometers between these two bad boys.

- Forbush Corners is open Thursday through Monday, and the trails are groomed daily.

  If you like groomed cross country skiing and lots of variety in the trail systems this, in my opinion, is arguably some of the best around the Great Lakes.

6

Hartwick Pines

winter is the right time for a hike on the Au Sable River

Hartwick Pines State Park Visitor Center (VC) trail system is a popular winter attraction, even with the other trail systems in the park.

The majority of park visitors migrate to the Visitor Center trails, especially the Old Growth Forest Trail and Aspen Trail for hiking, snowshoeing, and cross country skiing in winter. When the snow is adequate, they trek the 7-mile Weary Legs Trail. It can be busy, especially on weekends.

Photo: Adobe Stock

I personally like the Au Sable River Trail, which you will frequently have to yourself midweek. I don't recommend it for cross country skiing; there are lots of roots, and sometimes even wet, muddy areas. It's best to hike or snowshoe the trail when it's frozen and covered with snow.

The Au Sable River Trail offers a serene, 4-mile outing as it meanders along the East Branch of the Au Sable River, crossing it twice. It cuts through cedar swamps and stands of red pine, hardwood forests, and a beautiful virgin stand of eastern hemlock—you'll have to crane your neck in order to see the tops. Note the lack of undergrowth as you pass beneath the old giants.

About a mile before the end of the hike, you have a choice of a good climb up a ridge and back down, or take a much less strenuous route along an old two-track at the base of the ridge, rejoining the trail after it comes back down. Years ago, you used to have a view looking out over the river valley from the lofty perch, about 1,300 feet above sea level. Today it's all grown up and the trees have blocked the view. Cutting across the two-track through hardwoods offers a good chance to see deer if they are out.

Terrell's Trail Notes

T The park entrance road, off M-93, leads you to the VC parking area. The trailhead for the River Trail is off Bobcat Trail, on the other side of M-93. You need a Michigan Recreation Passport sticker on your car to enter the park.

T There are numbered posts along the trail that correspond to an interpretive guide—you can pick this up at the Visitor Center. From the parking area, the trail quickly crosses Bobcat Trail. In about a quarter mile, you come to an intersection with the loop trail. Head right, and in about a half a mile you'll come to the first river crossing. This beautiful, swift-flowing trout stream is crystal clear. A bench is strategically placed, offering a good view of the river. It's beautiful any time of year, but especially so in winter, when the overhanging trees along the bank are cottoned with white, fluffy snow. About the only sound you hear is the river water as it flows swiftly through the valley on its way to join the main stream.

T Once you cross the footbridge, you quickly move away from the river through bogs and a mostly pine forest. It's a little under a mile when you reach the second footbridge crossing the river. No bench, but it's still picturesque.

T After quickly crossing a cedar swamp, you arrive at numbered post 17, which marks the beginning of hiking underneath the giant hemlock stand. It's a Tolkien-like experience. In less than a half a mile, you'll come to the bottom of the ridge, and there's a sign indicating a good climb straight ahead, or an easier way to the left down a two-track. Once you intersect the regular trail again, it's about a mile of easy trail back to the parking area.

7

Corsair Trails

some of the best cross country skiing in Michigan

Corsair Trails, off Monument Road and 7 miles northwest of East Tawas, is one of the finest cross country trail systems in the Lower Peninsula.

Nestled among the beautiful Silver Valley hills and snow bowls, Silver Creek slices through the trail system, offering a picturesque backdrop. The system has 28 miles of groomed one-way trails that offer a wide variety of terrain, ranging from easy, rolling topography to hills with long downhill runs best skied with fresh tracks.

This area has long been a winter playground, dating back to the 1930s when the Silver Valley Winter Sports Park was created, complete with rope tow, toboggan run, and cross country skiing. It closed in the 1960s. The present-day trail system got its start in the 1970s. The Corsair Trail Council grooms and cares for the trails through an agreement with the Huron National Forest.

Gary Nelkie, who operates Nordic Sports in East Tawas, has been a driving force behind the creation of the trail system from the beginning, and still is 50 years later. He personally laid out much of the system, which has a nice rhythmic flow. When I skied with him in the 1990s, I remember him pointing out that he'd designed the hillier sections so that the downhill helped propel you up the next hill—it works well!

The majority of the trails are double-tracked, with a few trails on the Wright Lake section also groomed for skating. All of the loops are interconnecting and well-marked, with plenty of signage. They roll across open meadows, through sweet-smelling pines, towering hardwoods, and along the edge of gurgling streams.

"We find that the vast majority of our skiers prefer the double-tracked trails so they can ski side-by-side," Nelkie told me when we spoke recently. "We don't get many skaters. Our skate trails are not the nice, hard-packed trails like your Vasa Pathway. We don't have the equipment to achieve that type of trail, and skate skiers complain that it's too soft. We do what we can. The glide-and-stride skiers love our trails."

The Huron National Forest collects a daily use fee of $5 and a weekly fee of $15, payable at the trailheads in envelopes. The trail council depends on donations for grooming and upkeep.

Terrell's Trail Notes

🝓 Monument Road splits the trail in half. There are three trailhead parking areas: two off Monument Road, called Silver Lake, and Corsair; and one off Turtle Road, called Wright's Lake.

🝓 Both the Corsair and Silver Valley trails offer gentler terrain, rolling hills, and they skirt clear-running Silver Creek. There are some hills, but most are considered intermediate terrain.

🝓 My favorite loop is from the Corsair trailhead on the west side of Monument Road. The trail meanders along Silver Creek, crossing it a couple of times before heading up into the rolling hills and valleys that characterize the terrain on this side of the road. The constant up and down of the trail across the forested hills has a nice, rhythmic flow. It's approximately 6 miles around the loop.

🝓 The Silver Valley trailhead on the east side of Monument, offers trails that gently meander along Silver Creek for over a mile, then rise up into the surrounding hills. After climbing into an upland valley, the trail continues a long climb. The view from the top, overlooking the Gordon Creek Valley and surrounding hills, is a gem. The many eye-catching vistas around this loop are outstanding and worth the uphills. It's a little over 6 miles around the perimeter of this loop.

🝓 The Wright Lake loop off the Turtle Road trailhead offers some of the steepest terrain, with lots of hill climbs and some fast downhills. It also goes around two scenic lakes: Wright's Lake, named after some early settlers; and Lost Lake. It's a little over 7 miles around the outside of this loop.

🝓 Spend a couple of days exploring the trails. East Tawas offers lots of lodging and restaurant choices.

8

Pine River

a scenic, tranquil winter float

Winter float trips offer a different look at northern Michigan, offering solitude and quiet beauty along area rivers shrouded in snow.

I normally try to get in a winter raft trip every year, and was excited to learn that rafting trips were being offered on the Pine River for the first time during the winter of 2021. Pine River Paddlesports was conducting the trips.

The Pine has a reputation for being northern Michigan's feistiest river, with standing waves, rock beds, and plenty of riffles. Pine River Paddlesports has chosen a section on the upper river that is still fast, but without those rocks, waves, and riffles. It's still just as scenic as it flows underneath tall banks and forested hillsides devoid of any cottages.

The new rafting excursion has proven popular, according to Jacob Miltner, who along with his wife, Alaney, run the popular livery. 2021 marks their 50th year in the business, which was started by Jacob's father, Mark. The younger Miltner grew up in the business. It's the oldest livery serving the Pine River. The first float I did on the Pine was in the mid-70s, before moving to northern Michigan. It was a summer trip with friends from the Dayton, Ohio, ski club, where I lived at the time. We rented canoes from Pine River Paddlesports.

"We've been thinking of adding the winter schedule to the business, and this year, with all the interest in outdoor activities, decided to do it," Miltner explained as we floated down the river. "We've already got trips scheduled a month or two ahead. Weekends are proving to be very popular. Midweek isn't as busy."

Gliding along—at times ducking under branches of overhanging cedar—the snow-covered banks illuminate the darkly wooded shoreline. The only sound, when we were quiet, was the gurgle of rushing water as it swept along the gravely river bed and around obstacles, namely fallen trees and submerged logs. The water was clean and cold.

Since it was a midweek trip, my goldendoodle, Lulu, was able to go with me on the float—a nice addition that other area river floats don't offer. Her nose was constantly twitching with all the new river scents, and she got excited when a hawk took off from a tree along the bank above us. Eagles are often spotted along the river.

The float trip runs from Walker Bridge down to Lincoln Bridge, which takes about an hour and fifteen minutes. The spellbinding scenery makes the trip pass almost too quickly.

Terrell's Trail Notes

- The big difference between this and other winter float trips is that at the end, you have a choice of hiking back to the start or hitching a ride. The hike is along the beautiful Silver Creek Pathway, a loop hike along both sides of the river. Depending on the side of the river you choose, it's either a little over or a little under 2 miles. This hike between the Silver Creek Campground and Lincoln Bridge Campground flows up and down, offering you some stunning panoramic vistas up the length of the river from high ridges. At other times, you hike alongside the river: nice-sized trout hovering in the swift river current are sometimes visible just a few feet away. The Pine is one of the most popular trout fishing streams in Lower Michigan. The trail is well marked and easy to follow.
- The trips are guided. You can either help paddle, or let the guide do all the work while you enjoy the mesmerizing trip. The cost is $40 per person, and a group of four is required to book a trip.
- Pine River Paddlesports is about 90 minutes south of Traverse City. For more information on the location and scheduling a trip, you can log on to www.facebook.com/pineriverpaddlesports or call 231-862-3471.

9

Old Indian Trail

a winter outing through low dunes

One of my favorite Sleeping Bear Dunes hikes is the southernmost trail system along the National Lakeshore. Old Indian Trail is kind of an anomaly among the many scenic trails that abound throughout park, as it doesn't possess any spectacular overlooks, nor does it climb 400-some feet above the Lake Michigan shoreline.

It gained some fame years back when a park attendant was allegedly stalked by a cougar along a portion of the trail while out for a hike.

That incident prompted the National Park system to post a warning at the trailhead about possible cougar sightings and encounters.

Park officials called in one of their own wildlife experts to conduct an extensive survey during a winter in the early 2000s. They wanted to prove that cougars did exist within park boundaries. The study, however, found no evidence that big cats were roaming the park. Despite this lack of evidence, the warning signs remained up for a number of years. They were finally taken down just a few years ago, and replaced with warnings about ticks—a much more likely encounter, and one that should be taken seriously.

Old Indian Trail offers a really nice, easy pathway for a scenic ski or snowshoe hike during the winter months. The trail leads out to a beautiful, isolated beach among low dunes. The total distance is around 3.5 miles, with a couple of loops leading back to the deserted beach.

When you reach the beach along Platte Bay, you'll see few signs of civilization other than a couple of distant cottages to the south. Looking north, low dunes stretch as far as the eye can see along the bay. Sleeping Bear Dune looms above the water's edge, and looking out over the lake, you can clearly see the perched dunes on the west side of South Manitou Island.

The pathway was named Old Indian Trail because a portion of the trail was part of an established path that Native Americans used long ago when traveling along the coast between fishing camps.

You won't find an easier way to get to the beach and back in such a remote area of the National Lakeshore. When I was last there, the sun was a hazy shade of winter pale, and the stark landscape out along the beach, a perfect contrast.

Terrell's Trail Notes

🝆 The trailhead is located just off M-22, about 12 miles south of Empire. A sign for the trailhead is posted on the north side of the road. There are three trails that all converge on a short pathway leading to the beach and Lake Michigan.

🝆 A main trail leads from the trailhead back into the low dunes. It's .3 miles long, and both the Black Trail and Green Trail intersect it. The Black Trail—a 2.3-mile loop—works its way back into some low dunes with a few quick, steep hills. Nothing big—just quick ups and downs. The roller coaster effect is caused by ancient dunes that once marked the shoreline—a shoreline that was much higher several thousands of years ago.

🝆 The Green Trail—also a 2.3-mile loop—gently rolls through low dunes, without much climbing. Both trails intersect the pathway leading down to the beach, which is less than a quarter of a mile away.

🝆 It's best to visit on a windless day. It can really start blowing out along the beach, making the temperature level much less attractive, and sometimes downright uncomfortable.

🝆 This is part of the National Lakeshore system, and you will need a vehicle permit to park at the trailhead and access the trail system. Permits can be purchased at the Sleeping Bear Dunes visitor center in Empire. The best bet is to obtain an annual permit.

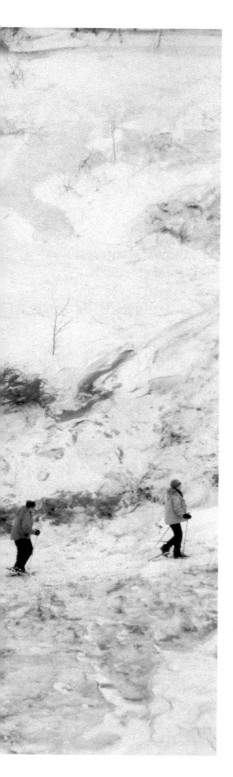

10

Old Baldy Dune

take your camera

Old Baldy may not be as well known as the Sleeping Bear, but it's found a good following among locals.

A perched dune—400-some feet above the Lake Michigan shoreline—Old Baldy looks out over Lake Michigan and the rugged, ice-encrusted shoreline far below. Located in the 3,600-acre Arcadia Dunes, it is part of the Grand Traverse Regional Land Conservancy stable of protected preserves and natural areas. The trailhead is off M-22, just south of the Joyfield Road intersection.

When you first climb into the dune, you can easily imagine you've climbed into a giant sundae bowl. Blowing sand mixes with snow to create maple- and caramel-colored swirls—it looks almost good enough to dip a spoon into! This is fine for snowshoeing, but it would create an abrasive surface for cross country skis.

There are a couple of trails leading to Old Baldy Dune. Snowshoe straight ahead across the dune, and you quickly come to a split in the trail. Continuing straight ahead, the trail climbs alongside a dune blowout to the top. You can see the Frankfort lighthouse far to the north, and massive sand dunes stretch along the ice-encrusted coastline. A portion of scenic Lower Herring Lake is nestled in a valley between dunes. Hopefully, you've picked a windless day so you won't freeze while drinking in this intoxicating panorama.

At the split, as you come back down, take the trail towards the lake. It leads through a notch in the dune to another steal-your-breath view of the lake and more perched dunes stretching south along the lakeshore as far as the eye can see. The contrast on a sunny day of steely-blue lake waters, bright blue sky, and the caramel-swirled snow is dazzling.

Pick a sunny day, grab your camera, and enjoy the view from the top. You won't be sorry. Summer is also beautiful here, but often much more crowded.

Terrell's Trail Notes

T The trails are well marked and easy to follow. From the trailhead parking lot, it's around .7 miles to the top, taking the most direct route. Head over to signpost 2, then on to posts 4 and 5 where you'll come to the cable steps leading up to the open dune. The out-and-back trip is around 1.5 miles.

T If you want to enjoy the longer woodland pathway, head over to post 3 and around to posts 4 and 5—it's a little over a mile longer this way to the top of the dune. Returning via the more direct route would make a round trip of 2.5 miles.

T Both ways are fairly easy. The first climb—which isn't long—is the steep cable steps. Once you're on the open dune, you still have another climb to reach the crown. It's not bad, but climbing through the soft snow and sand can be strenuous. Just take your time. There's a lot of scenery to enjoy. Coming back down out of the dune is a breeze.

T This is one of the easier snowshoe hikes leading to a spectacular overlook along Lake Michigan's dune country. Most of the Sleeping Bear Dunes National Lakeshore trails involve more climbing and long hikes.

11

Treat Farm Trail

a hidden gem

Some of the best views rewarding a snowshoe hike can be found along the coast in Sleeping Bear Dunes National Lakeshore. But those jaw-dropping views come with a price ... normally. Most of the coastal hikes aren't what I would call easy.

There is one outing along the National Lakeshore that is easier than most, though. The Treat Farm Trail has a very manageable climb, and is not a long trail. It's a round trip of about 1.5 miles, leading you to a breathtaking panoramic view from a bluff that follows the crescent of the Platte Bay shoreline.

The trail is known by locals, but you won't find many out-of-area visitors making the trek up to the old farm to enjoy the bluff views. For whatever reason, the National Park Service doesn't list the trail on its website among its popular hiking trails. For a long time, there wasn't even a sign by the Norconk Road trailhead. There isn't a designated parking area like other trailheads, either. You park along the road.

Set in an upland meadow tucked between a hardwood forest and a dune bluff known as Old Baldy, the Treat Farm is all that its name implies. It's one of my favorite hikes along the National Lakeshore, a real "treat." A snowy winter makes it even more so, with trees draped in snow and a white blanket covering the upland meadow.

It's about a half a mile up to the homestead—which does involve a moderate climb, but it's much easier than the park's best known overlook trails at Pyramid Point, Bay View Trail, Alligator Hill, the Dune Climb, or Empire Bluff.

An 1880 farmhouse, a restored barn on its original foundation, and some outbuildings are the first things to come into view on top. The homestead sits in an upland meadow under the towering Old Baldy Dune. You pass under the dune along the meadow trail leading to the bluff.

The farm was abandoned in the early 1900s because the sandy soil proved unfit for farming. They also had to transport water up to the farm for household and livestock.

The trail across the meadow from the homestead to the bluff is readily visible and easy to follow. Views stretch as far as you can see in either direction.

A retired park ranger friend once told me that he considered the Treat Farm Trail to be one of the park's "hidden gems." I couldn't agree more. It's also a delight during other seasons, including spring, when wildflowers light up the forest, and in the fall, when colors blaze across the hillside.

Terrell's Trail Notes

- Norconk Road, off M-22 south of Empire, dead-ends at the trailhead to the Treat Farm. You park along the road, go around the gate, and it's a half-mile snowshoe hike up through the forest to the collection of old farm buildings—all well over a century old. You could cross country ski it, but the old farm road is rutted and unsafe, in my opinion.

- From there, it's less than a half a mile across the open field to the lakeshore bluff. The trail passes beneath Old Baldy. There are no trail markings, but the well-worn pathway is easy to follow. Breathtaking views of secluded beaches, an often ice-encrusted shoreline, and Lake Michigan stretching as far as the eye can see unfold from the high bluff. Looking south, the coastline curves from the crescent of Platte Bay all the way north to Frankfort. Empire Bluff is just north of you.

  It's a panorama that never gets old at any time of year.

12

Kehl Lake

hike through old-growth pine and hemlock

Years ago, I discovered the Kehl Lake Natural Area on a guided hike with Brian Price, who was then executive director for the Leelanau Conservancy. I've been back many times since, just to enjoy a quick hike around this peaceful preserve. And, I've discovered that winter is my favorite time to visit.

The trails aren't long—a little over 2 miles—which makes a nice, quick hike any time of the year. Even more so when up to 200 species of birds have been seen migrating along this Lake Michigan flyway. Bear and bobcat tracks have also been spotted in the area. Old-growth white pine and towering hemlocks guard and shelter the trail. I like the winter, though, because I normally have it to myself.

Kehl Lake was once a summer gathering spot for the Ottawa and Chippewa tribes, prior to the arrival of the settlers. A large, decaying "marker" tree with a distinctive kink stands in an open spot along the south lakeshore, marking the camping spot. You come upon it fairly quickly after entering the forest on the trail. It's also the first good glimpse you have of the small, scenic lake.

Around 1860, the Kehl family built a cabin and homesteaded a 160-acre farm along the south side of the lake. That area is made up mostly of wetlands, lowland hardwoods, and conifers. The soil drained poorly and was unsuitable for farming, so much of the land was not disturbed—which also accounts for the old-growth pine and hemlock forest.

"Many of these trees are well over a century old," Price explained. "Some of the eastern white pines that we see from the trail are thought to be over 200 years old."

According to the longtime land preservationist, the forest has remained unaltered by human activity. "The trees aren't as big as old-growth white pines you see at Hartwick Pines State Forest because fluctuating water conditions have never allowed one species to dominate the landscape long-term. White pines adapt to a variety of growing conditions and soil types, which is why the species has existed since the days of dinosaurs," Price said, pointing to the trees.

While these trees don't reach the heights of ancient white pines elsewhere in Michigan, their trunks can be ample, up to

four feet in diameter. Even so, they were considered stunted, and were thus spared the fate of most white pine during the lumbering era of the late 1800s in Leelanau County.

I like standing by the lake and wondering what an early encampment of Native Americans would have looked like and what they would have been doing. Many of the old trees would have been here during those last campsites. It's like a walk back in time.

Terrell's Trail Notes

🚩 The trailhead is about 4 miles north of Northport on Kehl Lake Road. The trail winds quickly across an open meadow, heads into the old-growth forest, then down along the lake. The outer trail continues to a trail sign pointing to the viewing platform on the west end of the lake—a nice tranquil spot to enjoy the view. Now, head back to the trail sign and follow the trail on around; you'll pass many more ancient trees.

🚩 You'll come to an intersection with a spur leading to the Old Birch Loop, or you can head back to the parking lot. The Old Birch Loop leads you across more bridged wetlands and into hardwoods and fields in the upland section of natural area.

🚩 Total distance for both loops is a little over 2 miles.

Lake Ann Pathway

a winter favorite

Located outside the tiny hamlet of Lake Ann, this compact DNR pathway is one of my favorite winter trails.

The pathway appeals to a wide variety of trail users. Cross country skiers have long used the trail system, but in the last couple decades, snowshoeing has also become a popular mode of trail travel.

This beautiful wooded pathway is tucked in between Lake Ann, the Chain O' Lakes, and the Platte River. Reynolds Road—where you'll find the parking lot—divides the pathway into two different trail systems. Both are equally scenic—it just depends on how much of a workout you want.

The west side of the road is close to 4 miles of challenging trail, with several hill climbs and fast downhills. The rolling trail passes along a series of small lakes, active bogs, and the Platte River before climbing large bluffs above the river.

On the east side of the road—where the parking lot is located—the mellow trail glides along the Platte River and the shore of Lake Ann in slightly under 2 miles.

The first small lake you come to along the western trails—called Shavenaugh Lake—was named after an old settler who, in the early 1800s, lived in a cabin there. An old legend claims he is buried in an unmarked grave underneath one of the towering pines on the shore opposite from the trail.

The other small lakes on the trail were once interconnected and are commonly called the Chain O' Lakes—which was also the name of the pathway on old trail maps. It was changed by the DNR years ago to the Lake Ann Pathway, more reflective of its location. There's also a state campground here, which is not open in the winter. A recreation passport sticker is required on your vehicle to enter the trailhead parking area.

For a quick, scenic ski or snowshoe hike, which can be as vigorous as you want to make it, the Lake Ann Pathway is one of the best choices around Traverse City.

Terrell's Trail Notes

T If you want to ski or snowshoe the roller coaster-like west trail, cross the road from the trailhead and proceed to post 5. Head around the loop counterclockwise towards post 6. The trail system sets the tone with quick hills, before winding down alongside the small lakes. From there, it climbs to posts 6 and 7. At both posts are shortcut trails avoiding the hilly 2-mile section down to the Platte River and back up.

T Posts 7 to 9 offers the longest, hilliest section of the trail system, but also one of the most scenic. From tall hills, you drop down along the wild, unspoiled river. The trail continues its roller coaster to post 10, skirting high bluffs and offering peeks of the river far below. Head back to post 5 and the trailhead.

T To take the shorter, easier eastern trail system, head to post 2 through post 3 and around to post 4. From post 3, the trail begins a long gentle descent down to the picturesque river edge. There's a bench, so you can stop and enjoy this scenic spot. In winter, the fresh mantle of white covers trees and logs outlining the dark, swift-flowing river.

T At post 4, there's a shortcut up the hill back to post 3—if you want to skip the last mile. To continue around the trail, proceed along the panoramic lakeshore before climbing back into the hills and returning to the trailhead.

14

Lone Pine and Keystone Rapids

**a dashing river
and bluff views**

On a sunny day in early December, when winter has made an early appearance, the weather shouted for me to get out and enjoy the moment. Sunshine is a rare commodity in December—so I like to seize the moment and enjoy it.

On this day, there wasn't enough snow for cross country skiing, but it covered the ground and created a perfect backdrop for a winter hike along the Boardman River, south of town on the Keystone Rapids and Lone Pine Trails, part of the Grand Traverse Educational Reserve.

This is a great spot to enjoy a quick outing any time of the year, as the Reserve's trails highlight the power of the river. The dark ribbon of water defined by a white, snowy landscape evokes a mesmerizing contrast on its never-ending rush through the valley—especially now that the dams have been removed. I do enjoy winter more than any other season along these trails, because other seasons—especially summer—are so much busier with trail users and river users.

On this trail, you pass through a remnant of what was once the Keystone Dam—which washed out in 1961. That changed the course of the river and created the rapids—the only natural Class II rapids in the Lower Peninsula. The half-mile trail along these rapids offers many views of the river dashing over and around boulders. There are also some up-close views down along the river, and other views from platforms along bluffs. You can almost feel the velocity of the river in its white water.

On this particular sunny day, I combined the two trail systems—which are connected—for a winter hike of a little over 3 miles. My goldendoodle, Lulu, was happy when we met a couple of other people enjoying the day with their dogs, too.

Terrell's Trail Notes

T I like to begin my hike at the Oleson Bridge Trailhead, off Keystone Road and just before the intersection with River Road. It's a quick hike down to post 21 along the river. Hike the out-and-back Keystone Rapids Trail next and enjoy the many views of the powerful rapids.
As it is relatively close to Keystone Road, you do hear traffic noise along some portions of the trail. Other portions are blissfully quiet—except for sounds of the rushing river.

T When you get back to post 21, cross the bridge and proceed over to post 24 where you can pick up a half-mile loop trail over to post 25 and back. This portion of the trail has many wonderful river views, some winding through land that was once Boardman Pond. Back at post 24, head to post 20, which you passed starting out. This time, though, head over to posts 18 through 16, where the Lone Pine Trail—which you picked up at 17—ends. Backtrack to post 18, where there is another platform hanging out over the river, offering more breathtaking views. From there it's over to post 19 and back to the trailhead parking.

T The total distance is a little over 3 miles, but I can't count the number of river views you get.

15

Muncie Lake

a single-track heaven

I remember years ago, pausing at the bench overlooking the Boardman River on the back part of the Muncie Lakes Pathway to watch a pair of cross country skiers plummet down the trail off a large ridge above the river. Both had big smiles as they approached me.

"What a great trail system," enthused the first skier to arrive. They were visiting the area from downstate. "It's beautiful. We just don't have consistent snow in our area, and tracked systems are almost nonexistent. What a treat to have a tracked trail close by, especially one as scenic as this one. It's just beautiful back in the woods, getting down to the river, and skiing back up along the ridges."

When it comes to classic, single-track skiing with no skating lanes, it doesn't get much better than Muncie Lakes Pathway. It's one of few in the region, and the only one on state land that I can think of.

When I first moved up here in 1979, the Traverse City DNR Field Office groomed here weekly, along with a handful of other state-land trails. That ended almost three decades ago, after severe cuts to DNR budgets. But, thanks to local skier John Heiam—who several years ago established a grooming fund—and a cadre of volunteers, Muncie Lakes has continued to provide great skiing.

That's the kind of loyal following this popular trail system has fostered. Single-track skiers love their sport. I personally like the quiet solitude and beauty of nature, without having much faster skate skiers blowing by—most of whom don't reply when offered a greeting.

Just about any day of the week during winter there will be vehicles in the trailhead parking lot off Ranch Rudolf Road. However, the 9-mile trail system easily absorbs skiers, spreading them out over various loops. A lot of the time—weekends being the exception—you probably won't see a soul.

Terrell's Trail Notes

▼ Muncie Lakes Pathway offers several loops of varied distance and difficulty levels. The total distance around the outside trail is just short of 9 miles. The trailhead parking lot is off Ranch Rudolf Road, about a mile west of the intersection with Rennie Lake Road.

▼ The first loop—following the signposts from 1 to 3, over to 12, and back— is the easiest. It's only a couple of miles of gently rolling terrain; a nice outing for novice skiers or just a quick ski.

▼ Touring out into the rest of the trail system will take you by quiet, frozen lakes and down along the swift-flowing Boardman River with some nice overlooks of the river and valley along the way. Beyond the first loop, there are three more loops of varied length.

▼ The 4-mile loop continues from signposts 3 to 4, over to 11, and back. It features some moderate rolling hills, forest and open terrain, and an overlook of the river at post 11.

▼ The 6-mile loop continues from posts 4 to 8, over to 10, the 11, and back. This segment meanders down along the scenic frozen lakes, staying mostly in forested terrain with a couple of larger hills.

▼ The most difficult section of trail—also one of the most scenic—is the portion from posts 8 to 9 and back to 10, which also completes the 9-mile outside loop. The pathway tumbles off a steep ridge down along the river to post 9, then begins the long climb back up the ridge to post 10, where you're a little over 2.5 miles from the parking lot.

16

Vasa Headwaters

shorter scenic outings

The Vasa Headwaters Trail has always been one of my favorite area trails for a quick scenic hike or cross country ski. It's accessed—along with the longer 10K and 25K trails—from the Vasa Pathway trailhead off Bartlett Road. It's a microcosm of the longer, hillier trail, but it still offers a good workout in a much shorter distance.

It was devastating to see the damage done to this trail with the onslaught of the 2015 storm. It looked like a war zone, with trees lying in all directions and the thick woods that had bordered the trail gone.

Jim Heffner, who has worked tirelessly taking care of the Vasa Pathway for the past 25 years, took me around the new trail on a May morning in 2000 to show me what they had created. The Vasa had a well-deserved reputation for being a challenging trail, but Heffner developed an easier version for beginning and intermediate skiers. Hikers and mountain bikers can also enjoy this for a quick outing.

While the Headwaters Trail looks quite a bit different today—with all the open areas where woods were simply blown down—it's still a pretty trail that offers nice seclusion for cross country skiing. You ski along the west branch of Acme Creek, up into the hills above the creek, then around a long, wooded ravine where springs form the headwaters of Acme Creek. There are benches along the creek and along the trail above the headwaters.

That storm actually exposed a ticking time bomb. There were many old aspen trees—well beyond their life span—that should have been taken out years ago. But, anti-logging sentiments over the years prevented that. Many of those trees came down along the Headwaters Trail, and also took down the oaks, maples, and pines around them. It left a mess.

The storm-damaged trees taken during the salvage operation have resulted in a sustainable, healthy, beautiful forest for the future. Mother Nature recovers quickly. This is a scenic trail that frequently offers wildlife sightings, especially in the early morning and late afternoon.

Terrell's Trail Notes

T The trail starts out following the Vasa Pathway for about the first half mile. At the first signed intersection, the Headwaters Trail takes off to the right, climbing up a fairly long hill. After the climb, you'll have an equally long, fun downhill run that isn't steep. At the bottom of that run, there is a quick crossover trail to the Vasa Pathway, and shortly beyond that cutoff is a not-so-easy-to-see trail that leads over to a bench along swift-flowing Acme Creek—a beautiful spot.

T The trail continues back up into the hills above the wooded headwaters ravine. More benches will appear along the trail, offering different looks at the ravine from above. At the last bench along the trail, before returning to the Vasa Pathway, you can see the springs below.

T On your return to the trailhead parking lot, you'll follow the Vasa Pathway above the east side of Acme Creek, then cross on a wooden bridge after a quick downhill run. There's a bench to enjoy the view of the gurgling creek. It's surprising to see how quickly Acme Creek forms from the springs.

17

Vasa Snowshoe Trail

explore the beginning of Acme Creek

A new snowshoe trail—
opened a few years ago at
the Vasa trailhead off Bartlett
Road—is a gem, and most of the
time you won't even notice that
the relatively busy cross country
pathway is in close proximity.
The times I've snowshoed here
it's been golden silence with
just the sound of my snowshoes
swishing through the snow
and gurgle of swift-flowing
Acme Creek.

The scenic trail—which follows the West Branch of Acme Creek—offers a chance to see salmon in the creek, occasionally hear barred owls, spot deer coming down to the creek for a drink, as well as pileated woodpeckers, red-shouldered hawks, and ruffed grouse. All call the area home.

It's also a chance to explore the wetlands along the creek and the springs in the valley between the Vasa Pathway and Headwaters Trail, as the snowshoe trail traces the beginnings of Acme Creek's West Branch. You can often hear skiers passing—mostly out of sight—well above you.
A couple of benches on the trail have been strategically placed for breathtaking stops: one along a scenic section of the creek, and the other above the springs looking down at the headwaters.

Sections of this trail are only available in winter due to soggy wetlands, gnarly roots, and lots of biting insects during other times of the year. Catch a glimpse into a portion of our natural world that's not often available.

Terrell's Trail Notes

T The snowshoe trail—which starts right behind the maintenance barn at the Vasa trailhead off Bartlett Road—is divided into three stacked loops that total around 3 miles. Follow the "snowshoe blazes" painted on trees along the trail.

T The first loop—and the longest at around 1.5 miles—is the easiest. It heads down into the creek valley at the first intersection. Follow the loop to the left and across a log bridge. The trail meanders up and down a ridge, then heads back down into the valley and across the creek on the Vasa Pathway bridge. Make sure you stay out of the skier's way while crossing the bridge. The loop returns along the west side of the creek, staying mostly in close proximity and offering great views of the rushing water—plus, the chance to spot salmon.

T Continue on to the second and third loops on the other side of the Pathway. This trail follows the creek up to its headwaters. The first loop, about .75 miles, follows the west side of the creek, initially staying in close proximity until meandering up and down a ridge with the Headwaters Trail within view. Then, it heads back down, where a log bridge crosses the creek and the loop returns along the east side to the Vasa Pathway bridge, rejoining the first loop.

T The third short loop—a little over .25 miles—is the most difficult. It quickly climbs to the top of the ridge, emerging along the Headwaters Trail as it circles around the springs in the deep valley. A bench is perched on the edge of the trail, offering a nice view of the springs. The loop then quickly descends into the valley, crossing another log bridge as it goes around the springs and back along the east side of the creek. I find it amazing how quickly the springs gather strength to become a swift-flowing, full-fledged creek—which it does by the time you reach the log bridge crossing for the second loop.

18

Maple Bay

a winter hike along Lake Michigan

One of my favorite go-to spots for a winter beach hike is Maple Bay Natural Area between Acme and Elk Rapids.

The trailhead is just off U.S. 31. You take the drive by Grand Traverse Regional Land Conservancy's Maple Bay Farm house and barn. You can hear busy road traffic from the parking area, but once on the trail that quickly drops down a bluff, the noise of bustling vehicles disappears.

The trail out to the lakeshore takes you through a kind of enchanted, winter forest setting when the trees are cottoned with snow and the bright, blue skies overhead are visible through treetops. Proceeding down the trail, you'll notice many large, toppled-over trees cut up along the footpath. That's the aftermath of the 2015 windstorm that tore through our area. A plaque along the trail offers details.

The blue lake waters appear through the trees as you head up the trail paralleling the shoreline. The trail continues north, allowing more lake views. Some have strayed from the trail and hiked along the frozen lakeshore. The surface can be uneven, so be careful if you choose to do that.

There's something about icy landscapes that can be both intimidating and irresistibly captivating. The scenery, the silence of winter, the briskness of the air, and arctic-like patches of ice and land blend together to create a kind of magical frozen landscape. I'll stop, linger, and enjoy that view, but mostly keep moving along to avoid the cold. According to my fitness tracker, I hiked around 3 miles, venturing north to the edge of Petobego Pond, then back south to the southern edge of the natural area. All of the trails are out-and-back.

I have also hiked here on gray winter days. It can be just as appealing, especially if the shelf ice is lower and the waves have coated logs and underbrush with ice along the shore.

The trend with more people accessing area trails is continuing into 2021, especially when the winter has been mostly mild. Trailhead parking areas on weekends are busy. Midweek is a better choice.

Terrell's Trail Notes

T It's a short hike to signpost 1, and an even shorter hike straight ahead leads to open beach area. But, I like to head right (north) at post 2, along the shoreline. It's about a half a mile to post 5, then continue ahead for Petobego Pond. It's close to a 2-mile hike, out-and-back, to the edge of the pond and back to post 2.

T The conservancy map indicates that a small stream empties from the pond into the bay. With Lake Michigan's high water, the pond today is a bay of the lake—all open water.

T The short hike from posts 1 to 3 is a nice stroll underneath a tall bluff. The trail leads over to a panoramic view south, down the bay from the natural area. It's a little over a half a mile out and back to post 1.

T If there hasn't been recent heavy snowfall, the trail will probably be packed enough to not require snowshoes.

19

Old Mission Point Park

uncrowded winter trails

Looking for scenic winter trails, uncrowded conditions, and not too far away from Traverse City? I've got the perfect spot for you. Old Mission Point Park—located at the tip of the peninsula— fills the bill.

There aren't any groomed trails, but they are often skier-tracked, and most of the time snowshoers stay off the ski tracks and walk beside them; a nice gesture.

The two trailheads—located off Murray Road and Ridgewood Road—are connected by a 3-mile trail crossing over the peninsula highlands, offering scenic views. When cross country skiing or using snowshoes for the trail, you can see bits of both bays in the winter, which you can't during other times of the year.

The trail between the two upper trailhead parking areas is a little less than 3 miles, with moderate rolling terrain. The trails—which often use old farm lanes lined by stately old trees—offer panoramic upland views stretching across open meadows and orchard land. You also pass through an old-growth forest near the tip of the peninsula.

Peninsula Township's Old Mission Point Park—which includes Lighthouse Park—contains around 560 acres. The state purchased the 500 acres of the orchard land in the 1980s to build a state park, but that never materialized. Lighthouse Park had a couple of miles of trails on 60 acres at the tip of the peninsula, but with a long-term lease on the unused state property, the township was able connect 5 miles of trails on the highlands with the shoreline trails. Altogether, the park now offers about 7 miles of trails for hiking, cross country skiing, and snowshoeing.

From the Ridgewood Road trailhead you can do about a 2-mile loop across open meadows and orchard land. It makes a great, quick outing—and if the snow isn't good for either skis or snowshoes, lace up some winter boots. It also makes a great, winter hike.

Pick a sunny day and enjoy. All seasons are beautiful here, but winter is the least crowded on trails.

Terrell's Trail Notes

🚩 From the Ridgewood Road trailhead, it's a fairly easy, 2-mile loop to ski or snowshoe hike. You have a short, out-and-back section at the start and at the end. An old farm lane heads north from the parking area, then curves gently downhill to the left. In a short distance, you come to the first intersection. All intersections have a trail map posted with a "you are here" marker.

🚩 I like to head right (north) at that intersection and proceed along a long, gentle, downhill run through a meadow-like area. Eventually, the trail turns sharply to the left, and in a short distance arrives at another intersection. For the 2-mile loop, head to the right (north) as you continue through open fields. You'll skirt woods before coming to another intersection. Proceed straight ahead, and it's a short distance to the next intersection.

🚩 Here you head left (south) up the hill—a decent climb—to a memorial bench marking a viewing area on top of a hill. You are about 270 feet above the lake level at this point, and can catch a glint of East Bay through the trees. The trail continues slightly downhill to the next intersection. Continue straight ahead, and in about a half a mile you'll arrive at the first intersection you came to when starting out. The trailhead parking lot is ahead.

🚩 Another option is to spot a car with a friend at both trailheads and ski, snowshoe, or hike the 3 miles between.

20

Maplehurst

scenic winter trail
overlooking Torch Lake

Having spent over 40 years hiking, snowshoeing, and cross country skiing our winter trails, I have my favorites—those trails I frequent more then others.

I can now add the Maplehurst Natural Area to that list.

The ridgeline trails at the natural area, which opened in 2019, have become a personal favorite, especially on sunny days. The bright, azure waters of Torch Lake glimmer through trees along the forested ridge, creating a pleasant contrast with the dark trees and snow-covered landscape. You see little of the lake when leaves are out.

Stately old trees surround the parking area and trailhead, which is one of the higher points around the area—around 230 feet above Lake Michigan. If it's a clear day, you can catch a distant glimpse of Elk Lake and Grand Traverse Bay. Looking south, you'll see scenic Lake Maplehurst, with trails leading down through a snow-covered meadow to the frozen lake. Other trails head off across a long, open meadow.

The 389-acre property offers ample opportunity for snowshoeing, cross country skiing, and plain old hiking, if the snow is thin. You probably want to restrict skiing to the trails along the edge of the long open meadow—over a mile in the back portion—and down to Lake Maplehurst. The terrain is mostly flat to gently rolling. You'll feel sequestered back in the undisturbed meadow.

The trails along the forested ridgeline would be difficult for skiing, with lots of quick ups and downs and turns. They flow along, hugging the bent and folded ridge for around 4 miles, offering plenty of Torch Lake views to keep you occupied.

The natural area also attracts many visitors in other seasons. Maplehurst Lake—a scenic, 60-acre upland lake—is a popular destination for summer visitors who enjoy hiking along lake trails and around the large open meadow on soft summer evenings.

Terrell's Trail Notes

T The marked trailhead is located off Waring Road, northeast of Elk Rapids.

T Normally well-worn trails, unless there's been recent snowfall, lead down to the edge of Lake Maplehurst, and another trail heads towards the forested ridgeline. The trail to the ridgeline quickly ducks into the woods.

T I like to do the trail in reverse order of the posted trail signs. I head over to post 10, where you either take the Ridge Trail or Stream Trail. I think the Stream Trail offers some of the best Torch views shimmering through the trees. It meanders up and down the irregularly shaped ridgeline, eventually going down to Torch Lake Drive, then back up through what used to be a small downhill ski area that closed in the 1950s.

T At post 5, you rejoin the Forest Trail, where you can either go straight ahead for about a mile as you wind back up the ridge to post 4, or head right for a little over a mile to reach the post. I prefer going right, where you encounter reminders that this ridge once housed a small downhill ski area, which I found fascinating.

You can still see where some of the runs were cleared, and where the T-bar lift lines came up the hill. They even placed some of the huge concrete blocks that acted as anchors for the lift pulleys along the trail for benches. I found it fun to imagine the line I would take down the steep ridge if I had just come up on a pair of downhill skis.

T It's a bit of a workout, but the trails have a nice flow to them. Between that and the constant eye-catching terrain you pass, you seem to forget the effort involved.

Sign at the top of Pyramid Point.

Index

About the Author

MIKE TERRELL has been an outdoor columnist for the *Traverse City Record-Eagle* since 1984. He has written articles for *SKI, Skiing, Ski Press, Cross Country Skier, Chicago Tribune, Booth Newspapers,* and *Detroit Free Press*. Since 1998, he has been Midwest Regional Editor for OnTheSnow.com and SnoCountry.com. He has authored two books on cross country skiing and mountain biking in northern Michigan, and he maintains memberships in the North American Snowsports Journalists Association (NASJA), Golf Writers Association of America (GWAA), and Michigan Outdoor Writers Association (MOWA). He was a nominee for the 2018 Northern Michigan Environmental Action Council environmental journalist of the year award.

Terrell can most likely be found hiking with one of his loyal fur companions. Over the years, he has had five dogs accompany him, mostly chocolate labs. His current companion—featured in the book—is Lulu, a goldendoodle. She has been with him since 2015. Growing up in central Indiana on a farm, he explored the fields and woods, and developed a love for hiking and being outdoors. After moving to northern Michigan in 1979, the outdoors became his passion. He has been writing articles and columns about it ever since.

Also from Mission Point Press

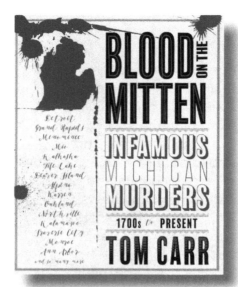

Michigan True Crime

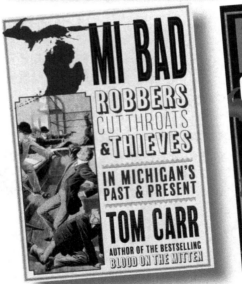

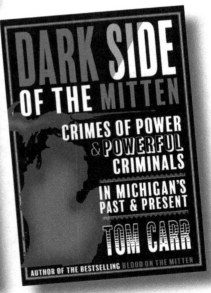

"Mild-mannered Midwestern Michigan is the land of lakeside cottages, auto industries, pasties—and murder? ... At times morbid and surprisingly colloquial, this collection serves to enlighten Michigan's present with the truth of its past and sheds a respectful light on the memory of its victims."

— Great Lakes, Great Reads, Historical Society of Michigan

Nature

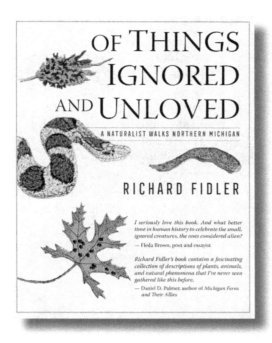

"Richard Fidler's book contains a fascinating collection of descriptions of plants, animals and natural phenomena that I've never seen gathered like this before."

—Daniel D. Palmer, author of *Michigan Ferns and Their Allies*

Children

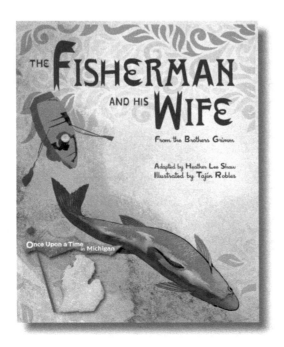

In this fable, a poor northern Michigan fisherman catches a magic fish.

When he tells his wife that he released the fish without asking for a reward, she makes it clear that

what the fisherman's wife wants, the fisherman's wife gets.

Local History

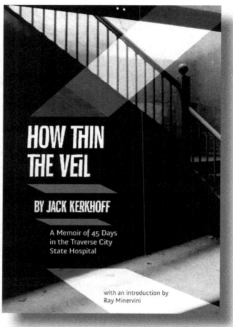

How Thin the Veil is a 45-day account of author Kerkhoff's treatment for depression. First published in 1952, the memoir shines a "hard-boiled" light on the mid-century conditions of patients of mental illness. Booze and cigarettes abound. Insulin-shock therapy was in vogue, as was what the patients called "eloctros."

The birth of drug therapy at the Traverse City State Hospital:

First there were cages and ice baths

Patients were animals

Then, there was electroshock

Patients were terrified

The lobotomy came next

And the soul was obliterated

Finally, the discovery that

INSANITY IS CHEMICAL

Michigan History

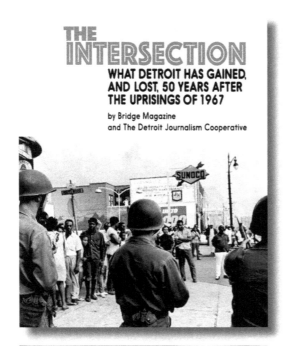

This collection of reporting from Bridge Magazine and The Detroit Journalism Cooperative is a bid to document how much has been gained in the half-century since the violence of 1967, and what has been lost.

Based on the award-winning journalism of Bridge Magazine, *Poison on Tap* provides a riveting, authoritative account of the government blunders, mendacity and arrogance that produced the lead-poisoned water crisis in Flint.

CPSIA information can be obtained
at www.ICGtesting.com
Printed in the USA
LVHW051525181121
703741LV00010B/941

9 781954 786219